THE GOLDEN GIFT

Breaking the Banking Cartel's Immoral Grip on Humanity

JS KIM

About the Author

JS Kim is the founder and current Managing Director of SmartKnowledgeU, a fiercely independent investment research & consulting firm with a focus on the Precious Metals of Gold & Silver. After being educated at an Ivy League school, JS finally received his true education regarding massive fraud and rigged markets in the financial industry when he accepted employment with a Wall Street Firm and as a Private Wealth Manager with one of the largest banks in America. After realizing that he would have to unlearn everything he had learned about financial markets in school, JS quickly made the decision to walk away from what he considered to be a morally and spiritually-bankrupt industry in 2005. In 2006, JS founded his own company, SmartKnowledgeU with a mission of (1) Restoring sound money to this world; and (2) Building wealth for clients by alerting and educating them to the immoral & fraudulent nature of our current banking & monetary system.

THE GOLDEN GIFT

Copyright © 2012 JS Kim. All rights reserved.
ISBN 978-0-9857827-3-3

"The few who understand the system will either be so interested in its profits or be so dependent upon its favours that there will be no opposition from that class, while on the other hand, the great body of people, mentally incapable of comprehending the tremendous advantage that capital derives from the system, will bear its burdens without complaint, and perhaps without even suspecting that the system is inimical to their interests."—The Rothschild banking family, to associates in New York, 1863.

JS KIM

CONTENTS

Chapter One...5
Unsound Money is the Root of All Economic
Discontent & Disorder in the World

Chapter Two..…………28
Ideological Subversion Transforms Lies into
Publicly Accepted Truth

Chapter Three………..71
The Gold Standard Ain't Broken &
It Never Has Been Broken

Chapter Four...............................……....…..............100
Fully Understand Monetary Debasement to Know
How to Protect Yourself During this Monetary Crisis

Chapter Five…….........................…...………….......108
The Solution Must Come From the People

Chapter Six………..125
A Modern Monetary Fable: Lost…with a Banker

Chapter Seven………….......…….........…..………..146
The Solution - Project Sound Money

Addendum…………….........................……………166

References………………....................…..………....177

THE GOLDEN GIFT

CHAPTER ONE

Unsound Money is the Root of All Economic Discontent and Disorder in the World

Inside this book is an idea that can spark a project that can revolutionize the world and ensure that the current global economic catastrophe of massive unemployment and currency devaluation that plagues nations in the Americas, Asia and Europe will be unlikely to ever repeat itself in the future. Not only would this idea impact humanity in a massively positive manner, from helping to alleviate poverty, restoring peace between warring nations, and destroying the conditions that give rise to terrorism, but it would also have profoundly positive implications for all of humanity, as it would expose the centuries long-fraud of the fiat-money based monetary system and global fractional reserve banking. Most importantly, it is an idea that could conceivably be implemented despite the strong opposition it would assuredly receive from Western governments and the global banking cartel. Before we can fully understand and appreciate the power of the idea contained inside this book, we must first take the time to understand the various participants that bankers have used to alter our perceptions about the massive financial frauds they impose upon all of humanity, from their immoral money creation monopolies called Central Banks to their Commercial Banking pawns that steal wealth from us through fractional reserve banking. We must then consider the various immoral mechanisms that bankers use to historically destroy our wealth such as their deliberate creation of price distortions in all capital markets that they falsely mislabel as "booms" and their consequent wealth theft mechanisms and deliberate contractions of capital markets that they falsely label as "busts." Finally, we must take the time to understand how bankers have polluted our political and academic systems to such a degree that we accept their altered, immoral, abnormal and distorted landscapes of business and financial concepts as our mind-numbing normality. I will explore all of these topics in The Golden Gift. Get ready for an eye-opening journey in which I will wipe away the false veneer of lies and perception that banksters have convinced us to accept as truth, and prepare yourself to re-construct every single belief that you have previously held about our banking and monetary system as we start the mind-blowing process of separating monetary lies from monetary truths.

Originally, a well-known global financial book publisher approached me about writing this book. However, after a brief period of thought, I decided to turn down the book deal because I wanted to ensure that I could write this book without any edits or limitations imposed by the commercialization process of a major book publisher and distributor. The solution I provide in this book to solve the immense Ponzi scheme that is our antiquated and immoral monetary system is not intended to be a "perfect" solution. As a solution, the idea I present in this book is only intended to spark conversations with your neighbors, friends, and family. It is intended to challenge your belief system about our current monetary system and to explain why our current monetary system is highly unethical, highly criminal, and enormously misunderstood. If your

THE GOLDEN GIFT

immediate reaction to this statement is one of disbelief, then you are exactly the person for whom I wrote this book. If you merely spend the couple of hours it takes to read this book, I guarantee you that your opinion about the banking system and its purpose will change immensely. Please note that I will soon be releasing a second companion book to this one that discusses a more easily applicable solution than the one I will discuss here in The Golden Gift. Though the solution I present to you in this book is not without logistic difficulties, I want to emphasize that it still can serve the extremely important purpose of initiating dialogue to expose the immorality of our current global banking and monetary platform. I believe that once all of us understand and can agree that our current global banking and monetary system is immoral, then the transition of moving from dialogue to action and implementation then becomes possible. That is why I wish to present my solution in two steps. The first solution is intended to initiate dialogue and the second solution is intended to initiate action. In no world, real or imagined, should a few thousand men be able to defeat 6.8 billion of us, if we, the 6.8 billion, unite. However, in order for us to unite, we must tear down all the lies that bankers have instructed us to believe are "truths" for the past century. So let us start deconstructing their lies now.

Bankers have incorporated lies about our monetary system into mainstream education and into everyday lore for centuries now. For this reason, lies about the monetary system are now readily accepted as the norm while the truth is viewed with skepticism. Were I to tell a newborn baby every year from the day he learned how to talk that reggae music was the music of the devil and that if he danced to reggae music, his soul would be vulnerable to possession, then I guarantee you that it would be very difficult to convince this person as a young man or young woman to enjoy reggae music. The process of repetition day after day, year after year, and decade after decade, is how bankers have convinced people to accept today's monetary system as legitimate and fair even though its acceptance is the equivalent of accepting slavery.

It was this same process of repetition by which the Catholic Church convinced the world that the sun circled around the earth for not several years, not a decade, but for more than 100 years! Though Copernicus had already written his heliocentric theory before 1514, more than a century later, Cardinal Robert Bellarmine of the Catholic Church was still refuting a heliocentric view of the solar system. Bellarmine stated:

"If there were a real proof that the Sun is in the center of the universe, that the Earth is in the third sphere, and that the Sun does not go round the Earth but the Earth round the Sun, then we should have to proceed with great circumspection in explaining passages of Scripture which appear to teach the contrary, and we should rather have to say that we did not understand them than declare an opinion false which has been proved to be true. But I do not think there is any such proof since none has been shown to me." (Source: Finocchiaro, Maurice A., Defending Copernicus and Galileo: Critical Reasoning in the Two Affairs, Springer Science & Business Media, 2010).

The Vatican placed Galileo under house arrest in 1633 until his death in 1642 after he published his views in the Dialogue Concerning the Two Chief World Systems and continued to persecute and arrest anyone that espoused the truth that Copernicus and Galileo bestowed upon humanity. In doing so, the Vatican convinced millions of people to believe their self-serving lies designed only to perpetuate their power and not to further any type of true honest religious enlightenment. Today,

THE GOLDEN GIFT

we have the exact same propaganda happening again in the financial world, with very prominent figures espousing lies to once again serve a political agenda that has nothing to do with truth.

In May of 2012, three very powerful global elitists, Warren Buffet and Charlie Munger of Berkshire Hathaway and Bill Gates of Microsoft, all denounced gold as having any type of value. Charlie Munger stated that *"gold is a great thing to sew onto your garments if you're a Jewish family in Vienna in 1939 but civilized people don't buy gold"*, a disingenuous statement that was followed up not a week later by an equally foolish statement by Bill Gates in which he urged people not to buy gold. Why would such prominent men issue such public, anti-gold statements?

The answer ironically is provided by one of these men's fathers, Howard Buffet. In 1948, more than 60 years ago, as a US Congressman, Howard Buffet stated that it was the right time to return to a sound money system backed by gold. Howard stated, *"Is there a connection between human freedom and a gold redeemable money? At first glance it would seem that money belongs to the world of economics and human freedom to the political sphere. But when you recall that one of the first moves by [Vladimir] Lenin, [Benito] Mussolini and [Adolf] Hitler was to outlaw individual ownership of gold, you begin to sense that there may be some connection between money, redeemable in gold, and the rare prize known as human liberty. Also, when you find that Lenin declared and demonstrated that a sure way to overturn the existing social order and bring about communism was by printing press paper money, then again you are impressed with the possibility of a relationship between a gold-backed money and human freedom...I warn you that politicians of both parties will oppose the restoration of gold, although they may outwardly seemingly favor it. Unless you are willing to surrender your children and your country to galloping inflation, war and slavery, then this cause demands your support. For if human liberty is to survive in America, we must win the battle to restore honest money."*

With great irony, we find ourselves in the 21st Century having to guard ourselves against lies spread by Howard's son, Warren, as Warren is willing to surrender the US to *"galloping inflation, war and slavery"* because unsound money, lies, fraud, and deceit are the principles of our unsound monetary system that enabled men like him to build his fortune. I also find with great irony that Charlie Munger, Warren Buffet's right hand man, denigrates gold for being *"unproductive"* and states that civilized people should invest in *"productive businesses"*. If Charlie Munger is sincere in his declaration, then he is advocating that anyone invested in Berkshire Hathaway stock should immediately divest of his or her investment.

According to Berkshire Hathaway's 2012 First Quarter report, nearly 90% of its revenues were earned from its insurance and financial business units, businesses that typically earn money by transferring money from all socio-economic sectors of society to itself. Talk about hypocrisy of the worst kind, Charlie Munger! If I were asked to compile a list of scams that most hurt growth and productivity in an economy, insurance businesses would definitely rank in the top ten. And what about those derivative products that Warren Buffet has publicly scoffed at with derision and coined as *"financial weapons of mass destruction"*? Apparently, Uncle Warren failed miserably in the transparency test as seems to be the case with all financial titans, as he was content to publicly

THE GOLDEN GIFT

denounce derivatives as "financial weapons of mass destruction" but to privately invest in them to the production of one billion dollars in revenues during the 1st Qtr of 2012.

Finally, if we look at the Wikipedia entry for Berkshire Hathaway, we will discover more ways Berkshire has used non-productive processes to produce self-serving gains that benefit no-one but Berkshire executives: *"Buffett has used the float provided by Berkshire Hathaway's insurance operations (paid premiums which are not held in reserves for reported claims and may be invested) to finance his investments."* In plain English, the previous statement exposes Buffet for using the sunken funds and capital expenditures of his insurance clients to bankroll the creation of more wealth for himself. Is this what you mean by being *"productive",* Charlie Munger? – to literally use other people's money to make more money for yourself while returning not a cent of interest to the people whose money you are using to do so?

One of Berkshire's largest insurance companies is Geico, an auto insurance company and an industry that I consider to be one of the biggest business scams ever. Over my driving career, I've literally paid tens of thousands of dollars of auto insurance yet have only been in one accident during my lifetime in which my insurance paid a few hundred dollars in claims. So in return for paying tens and tens and tens of thousands of dollars of insurance, I've received a couple hundred bucks in return for my investment? Talk about a rip-off and one of the worst corporate-win/consumer-lose propositions in the history of mankind?

In reality, auto insurance is just another form of socialism, as good drivers that never get in accidents subsidize the costs of poor drivers that experience frequent accidents. Furthermore, auto insurance executives use the premiums of good customers that never cost auto insurance companies a single dime to subsidize the costs of their high salaries and executive perks. But this should hardly be a surprise as people like Buffet that build wealth from socialistic tendencies strongly support tenets of Communism as well. Remember, Howard Buffet, Warren Buffet's father, reminded us that Lenin himself stated *"that a sure way to overturn the existing social order and bring about communism was by printing-press paper money."* Today, most people still do not know that one of the main principles of the Communist Manifesto is the *"centralization of credit in the hands of the state, by means of a national bank with State capital and an exclusive monopoly"* – the EXACT DEFINITION OF MODERN CENTRAL BANKS TODAY!

In fact, if one reviews the 10 major tenets of Communism as described here, (http://www.libertyzone.com/Communist-Manifesto-Planks.html), one is bound to discover that bankers and "free" governments have adopted many financial laws that more closely follow the principles of Communism rather than the principles of freedom. Why would governments and bankers collude to instill Communist principles as law in one's country? The answer is simple. Enforcement of these immoral monetary and financial tenets allow the ruling elite to control the remaining 99% of citizens in the country to such an extent that revolt against their immorality remains a slim threat.

In this book, I will prove to you beyond a shadow of a doubt that Charlie Munger has engaged in a public relations campaign to denigrate gold only because such spouted propaganda serves his interests and the interests of Berkshire Hathaway. A gold standard and a return to sound money would cause the greatest economic growth and production the world has ever seen, contrary to Charlie Munger's attempts to

THE GOLDEN GIFT

denigrate gold. A return to a gold standard would mean that men like Munger could no longer "game" the system for his own benefit to the detriment of the 99%, and that he would actually have to earn an honest living instead of merely parlaying other people's earnings and wealth into wealth for himself. And this is the REAL REASON men like Munger constantly denigrate sound money and try to break the ability of people to connect gold with financial freedom.

Before I continue, I want to clarify that the purpose of the above section is not to bash elitists like Warren Buffet, Charlie Munger, and Bill Gates that serve their own interests first and foremost over the interests of all humanity. The point of the above introspection is merely to point out to you that it is a huge mistake just to believe and accept something that a person in a position of authority states. In the world of endless propaganda that we live in today, it rather becomes a necessity to question everything that anyone in a position of authority instructs you to believe.

Likewise, I also encourage all of you reading this book to question everything I state in this book, even if you have been following me for years and consider me as a gold and silver "expert." I encourage all of you to research the points I make in this book before you decide to internalize them, as blind acceptance of information provided by any source today, no matter how authoritative, is bound to ensure that your belief system is littered with many more lies than truth.

Elitists always spout statements asking you to believe them, but you may note, they never encourage you to question them because their ability to successfully lord over all of us and their ability to rob us of our wealth depends on our lack of understanding regarding the mechanisms that they have put in place to accomplish their immoral goals. In order to make this book as accessible as possible, I decided to limit its length, so that the truth about our immoral monetary system may be learned quickly and spread far and wide. So without further ado, let's begin our journey of discovery in understanding the roots of this crisis as well as how we, the public, can fight back against the grave injustices being perpetrated by bankers through the global financial system today.

The root of every chord of economic discontent in every country in the world today has a common denominator - an unsound monetary system. The numerator may differ from country to country but the denominator is always the same. An unsound monetary system unjustly and immorally robs our wealth daily and prevents all of us from living the full, productive and creative life we all deserve. This maxim holds true whether you live in Nairobi, Dar es Salaam, Montreal, Berlin, Mexico City, Rio de Janeiro, Montevideo, Shanghai, Taipei, Amsterdam, New York, Santiago, Montevideo, London, Brussels, Bangkok or Tokyo.

An unsound monetary system perpetuates and facilitates poverty, terrorism, and wars. An unsound monetary system creates ever-increasing gaps in income between the rich and the poor, enabling the top $1/10^{th}$ of 1% of the world's richest families to unfairly manipulate financial & capital markets to create a bigger division in material wealth and income between themselves and everyone else. An unsound monetary system grants the families that control Central Banks absolute, immoral and unfair control over not only currency valuations, but also over real estate valuations, stock market valuations and commodity valuations.

An unsound monetary system grants the families that control Central Banks the unjust power to set artificial interest rates that could not exist in free markets, and consequently, the unjust power to deflate and inflate all asset valuations at will. This is precisely why the patriarch of the richest banking cartel in the world, Mayer Amschel Rothschild, stated, *"Give me control of a nation's money and I care not who makes the laws."* Former US President Woodrow Wilson (1913-1921) also stated the following in his book <u>The New Freedom: A Call For the Emancipation of the Generous Energies of a People</u>:

"A great industrial nation is controlled by its system of credit. Our system of credit is privately concentrated. The growth of the nation, therefore, and all our activities are in the hands of a few men who, even if their action be honest and intended for the public interest, are necessarily concentrated upon the great undertakings in which their own money is involved and who necessarily, by very reason of their own limitations, chill and check and destroy genuine economic freedom...We have restricted credit, we have restricted opportunity, we have controlled development, and we have come to be one of the worst ruled, one of the most completely controlled and dominated, governments in the civilized world-- no longer a government by free opinion, no longer a government by conviction and the vote of the majority, but a government by the opinion and the duress of small groups of dominant men."

This is precisely why the JP Morgans, the Rothschilds, the Rockefellers, the Warburgs, Citigroup, HSBC, et al, have fought so hard throughout history to ensure that today, all citizens utilize an unsound, unjust monetary system that provide them with capital markets that they can rig to their advantage to the detriment of the rest of humanity. Today, the families that rule Central Banks, perhaps no more than a dozen families worldwide, have precisely this power that enables them to set up a modern day feudal system where they are the lords and 99.9% of the world are their serfs. The poor and middle class and even the majority of the rich have no access to these mechanisms that allow Central Bankers and their Commercial Banking puppets the ability to create risk-free wealth for themselves year after year at the expense of the rest of humanity.

Today, it is no mystery why huge income disparities have formed between the top 1% of wealthiest citizens and the bottom 99% of citizens in every country and why the wealth gap between these two factions continue to widen at an alarmingly rapid schism. If you believe that the government will come to the rescue, you will be waiting for this rescue until the day you die, as all governments have been compromised by the global banking cartel and now run under the banking cartel's authority. Consider this article that ran on Marketwatch.com on February 9, 2012 about insider trading activity within the US Congress:

"The House of Representatives voted overwhelmingly Thursday in favor of legislation to curtail insider trading of securities by lawmakers and officials in the executive branch, including a provision inspired by an alleged trade made by the husband of House Minority Leader Nancy Pelosi."

The fact that the US Congress had to bring up for vote a separate law that defines a behavior as illegal exclusively for them that has already been illegal for all US citizens for decades implies one of two things:

THE GOLDEN GIFT

(1) the existing law does not apply to them; or
(2) members of US Congress are not US citizens.

As you can see by the absurdity of this situation, not only is the global financial system corrupt, but the "legal" system in many countries also is corrupt, having very little to do with governing morality and more to do with ensuring that those in power have access to special privileges that allow them to maintain their power. Laws that apply to 99.99% of all citizens of every country simply do not apply to a select 0.01% of the ruling elite. And who constitutes these 0.01% of ruling elite? The answer is the global banking cartel. This is why today we have absurd theater in the legal system.

Consider that with the exception of Bernie Madoff and Allen Stanford, the US "Justice" Department has prosecuted, tried and sentenced virtually zero bankers for their criminal acts compared to the savings and loans fraud of the 1980s in the US that led to 1,100 prosecutions and more than 800 bankers being sentenced to jail. So why today does the government spend millions of dollars and waste thousands of hours on trying to prove former ace Boston Red Sox pitcher Roger Clemens guilty of steroid and human growth hormone use, a relatively victimless act (unless you consider striking out baseball batters a crime) sans the harm to which he has subjected his own body, but not a single penny or a single second trying to bring thousands of criminal bankers to justice? The answer, of course, is that if you control the money, as the bankers do, then you also control the legislation.

The fact that virtually no bankers have gone to jail for absurdly criminal acts that have ruined millions of lives is tantamount to Mexican drug lords that never face justice in Mexico. In Mexico, drug lords bribe police, legislators and judges to ensure that they remain free to do as they please, just as US bankers have bribed police (JP Morgan's $4.6 MM "donation" to the NYPD in October, 2011, for example), US Congress and the Supreme Court.

Consider that the top 1% of American households captured nearly 70% of all income gains between the years of 2002 and 2007. During this same period, the bottom 90% of American households was only able to capture a piddling 12% of all income gains. An updated study for the two-most recent years following the 2008 global economic crisis illustrates that this trend has grown more absurd and become even more concentrated at the upper echelons of wealth. From 2009-2010, an astounding 93% of all income growth was captured by the wealthiest 1% of Americans, ***with nearly half of all income growth of the top 1% captured by only the top 0.01% of wealthiest Americans!*** This left 99% of Americans to fight for 8% of all remaining income growth from 2009 to 2010 in order to survive. Hardly a level playing field in the home of the brave and land of the free, right? But the bankers did not set up our modern banking system to be fair or free. They set it up so that they could pillage and plunder everyone else's wealth for their own benefit.

This obscene trend has occurred for a simple reason. The top bankers in every country, due to our current immoral fraudulent monetary system, not only have the ability to manipulate asset prices in all capital markets up and down at will, but they also have perfect, uncompromised knowledge of the timing of the rise and fall of asset prices for nearly all major global assets (Source: Feller, Avi and Chad Stone, 2009. Top 1 Percent of Americans Reaped Two-Thirds of Income Gains in Last Economic Expansions. Income Concentration in 2007 Was at Highest Level Since 1928, New Analysis Shows.

THE GOLDEN GIFT

Retrieved May 2012 from *the Center on Budget and Policy Priorities* website:
http://www.cbpp.org/cms/index.cfm?fa=view&id=2908,
and Shaw, Hannah and Chad Stone, 2012. Incomes at the Top Rebounded in First Full Year of Recovery, New Analysis of Tax Data Shows Top 1 Percent's Share of Income Starting to Rise Again. Retrieved May 2012 from *the Center on Budget and Policy Priorities* website:
http://www.cbpp.org/cms/index.cfm?fa=view&id=3697).

The majority of people in the world do not understand that Central Bankers deliberately enforce unsound monetary principles in every country to unfairly manipulate capital markets while they simultaneously ensure that the majority 99% of income earners in their respective countries will never be able to participate in receiving the same endless and effortless bounties that they perpetually deliver to themselves. To ensure ignorance of the principles that govern capital markets worldwide today, bankers have used their fraudulent monetary system to assert their enormous influence over the business curriculums of institutional educational systems and mainstream media distribution channels worldwide.

After all, if a family like the Rockefellers, who are shareholders of the US Federal Reserve, want a billion dollars, all they have to do is ask the US Federal Reserve to create it out of thin air and then they have a billion dollar bribery pool available to them to distribute among educational and media institutions. It literally is as simple as that. Since there are zero limitations on how much paper money of any kind, US dollars, Euros, Pound Sterlings, Yen, Yuan, etc. can be created under our current unsound monetary system, and there is zero accountability of Central Banks to publicly disclose for whom and for what institutions worldwide they create money, as absurd as this sounds, no one in the world can really prove or disprove such an event if and when it happens.

It is through the formal global education system that bankers have spread the lies that ensure people's ignorance on a wide scale. It is through the formal global education system that bankers have been able to reshape the belief systems of billions worldwide to include false and erroneous concepts regarding the inner workings of global monetary and capital markets. There are many people complicit in this web of deceit including Chancellors of the Exchequer, Treasury Secretaries, Finance Ministers, Presidents, Prime Ministers, and prominent university presidents and business school professors. Though these people do not control the monetary system, because bankers grant and award them their positions of power, they willingly participate in the big lie about the monetary system. I discuss and document the link between bankers and education more thoroughly in my companion book <u>The Bankers' Secret Plot to Bankrupt the World & How We Can Stop Them!</u>

There are only two reasons why bankers have unanimously agreed upon our current monetary system:

(1) It provides them with a mechanism to artificially manipulate the prices of all assets up and down at will; and
(2) It provides them with a mechanism (inflation) to silently rob people of their wealth in perpetuity and thus, a method to keep people financially downtrodden and unable to revolt against them.

If you are still having a difficult time believing that these concepts are true, please consider the following framework for digesting information as outlined by genius Leonardo da Vinci.

THE GOLDEN GIFT

Da Vinci observed that *"all our knowledge has its origins in our perceptions"*. Consequently, he concluded that *"Anyone who conducts an argument by appealing to authority is not using his intelligence; he is just using his memory."* This framework for learning explains why it has been such a difficult road to convince the masses of the utter immorality and criminality of the fractional reserve banking system today. If we *"perceive"* the banking system today to be just because we have been told by an *"authoritative"* figure to believe this, then we will believe this. However, the moment we cease accepting as *"fact"* statements about the monetary and banking system that *"authoritative"* figures have instructed us to believe, then this is the moment when our eyes will finally open and we will finally awaken to the harsh truth and the real purpose of our banking and financial system.

I have noted that over the years, as I've extolled the virtues of sound money and the importance of the use of gold (and silver) to the re-establishment of a banking system that is honest and just, people have unsuccessfully attempted to refute me merely by repeating the arguments of authoritative figures like Warren Buffet, Bill Gates, Paul Krugman and Ben Bernanke without the introduction of a single original thought. Often the reasons people dismiss my arguments are as simple as *"Oh, so you know more than Warren Buffet, you idiot. Are you a billionaire?"* as if wealth were directly correlated to intelligence and reason. If this were the case, then every wealthy drug lord and brutal dictator in the world would be Renaissance men and the greatest thinkers of our time. And in the rare instance when someone actually engages me in debate, I often recognize his or her argument as one made by an authoritative figure like Krugman or other sophists and not as an original argument. Thus, they have fallen victim to da

Vinci's criticism of engaging in debate not through the use of critical intelligence but through the regurgitative use of memory only.

Though I have supplemented my arguments with arguments of other known figures in this book, I have only done so in an effort to capture the attention of skeptics, and because I know that our global educational system has conditioned people to give more credibility to well-known public figures than to people not as famous. However, I have reached my own conclusions about the immorality of our current monetary and banking system through researching all facets of the monetary system, not through researching the opinions of known figures. In fact, I have heavily researched the opposition viewpoint as well and will present my own arguments and logic that explain the immorality of our current monetary system later in this book. It is also why I encourage everyone to not just accept the information I present in this book but to dissect the information for yourself and to reach your own conclusions. This is the only way we can possibly sharpen our critical thinking skills and become better, and eventually, great thinkers.

Thus, if you disagree with the points I have thus far made in this book, please give yourself a chance to hear an alternate viewpoint that may forever change the way you view the role of money in your life. It is said that the most intelligent of women and men may not agree with an alternate line of thought presented to them, but that all intelligent people will at least consider the evidence presented to them before passing any judgment as to its veracity or its deceptiveness. If you finish reading this book and still do not believe that our current monetary system is fraudulent, unsound, and criminal in nature, then at a minimum, by finishing this book, you will

THE GOLDEN GIFT

have given yourself a fighting chance to truly understand the massive financial fallouts and "black swans" that will occur in the future when the second phase of this monetary crisis likely commences at some point in 2012, 2013 or in the year beyond. And by understanding why they are happening, you will have provided yourself with the opportunity to react properly to them.

The reason that the great majority of us do not understand why our current monetary system is unsound, immoral, and detrimental to our freedom and financial health is because bankers have successfully conditioned us for over a century to accept statements of authoritative figures at face value. They have accomplished this not only through the enormous influence they wield within our institutional academic system but also through their control over the mass media. Blindly trusting any leader in a position of authority, as bankers desire all of us to do, is an enormous mistake. In fact, a simple investigation of public statements issued by many of the most powerful figures in our global monetary system would reveal startling contradictions and grave inconsistencies, but yet even the smartest among us often are too lazy even to conduct this simple exercise. For example, just watch some of the videos listed in the Reference Page at the end of this book to understand the lies that bankers regularly tell us is "truth".

In 1967, former US Federal Reserve Chairman Alan Greenspan, arguably one of the most powerful bankers in the history of banking, stated the following in an essay titled *"Gold and Economic Freedom"*, an essay that was earlier printed in the Objectivist newsletter in 1966 as well as in Ayn Rand's 1966 book Capitalism, The Unknown Ideal:

"In the absence of the gold standard, there is no way to protect savings from confiscation through inflation. There is

no safe store of value. If there were, the government would have to make its holding illegal, as was done in the case of gold. If everyone decided, for example, to convert all his bank deposits to silver or copper or any other good, and thereafter declined to accept checks as payment for goods, bank deposits would lose their purchasing power and government-created bank credit would be worthless as a claim on goods. The financial policy of the welfare state requires that there be no way for the owners of wealth to protect themselves. This is the shabby secret of the welfare statists' tirades against gold. Deficit spending is simply a scheme for the confiscation of wealth. Gold stands in the way of this insidious process. It stands as a protector of property rights. If one grasps this, one has no difficulty in understanding the statists' antagonism toward the gold standard."

Yet two decades later, in the very year Alan Greenspan became US Federal Reserve Chairman in 1987, gold peaked at $500 an ounce. For the next 14 years, gold suffered its longest and greatest decline in modern times under the very tenure of the man that had stated earlier in his career that gold price stability and freedom were inseparable. This fact alone should make you think. How could a man that once championed a stable gold price and freedom as inseparable reside over the longest period of decline in gold prices in modern history and one during which the price of gold plummeted by 50%? If you wonder why Greenspan executed a complete reversal in his views about gold and participated in gold price suppression schemes after he became a pawn of the Central Bankers, as the devil says, everyone has a price. I'll explain in this book, why the pre-US Federal Reserve Greenspan was right and why the Greenspan that sold his soul to the US Federal Reserve was wrong. More importantly, I'll present a possible solution to implementing a sound monetary system today that would forever end the Central Bankers' monetary enslavement of the people.

Before I continue, I want to provide a couple of references that explain why our current monetary system is fraudulent and unsound. There are numerous books already available that explain this topic very well so there is no need for me to regurgitate this information. Below are a couple of books I recommend to learn the truth about our current monetary system and how it truly operates.

<u>The Road to Serfdom</u>, by Friedrich Hayek
<u>The Theory of Money and Credit</u>, by Ludwig Von Mises

The purpose of this book along with my companion book <u>The Banker's Secret Plot to Bankrupt the World & How We Can Stop Them!</u> is to increase awareness of the inherent immorality of our current banking and investment system among the world's citizens and also to present a solution to our global monetary crisis. These are the topics I will address within this book the most fully. The most common complaint I've heard about critics of our monetary system from supporters of our current monetary system is a claim that critics complain about injustices without the provision of a solution. Frankly this is a lie, because many among us have presented various solutions and I will provide a proposed solution in this book as well.

Supporters of our current immoral monetary system also falsely claim that the system we use today, while highly flawed, is the best possible system that man can possibly invent, so we should learn to live with its flaws. In refutation of this ignorance, I will explain in this book why a precious metal-backed monetary system is the solution to our current global monetary woes, how such a system could feasibly be implemented, and why such a system would protect the salaries and savings of citizens worldwide even if "banksters" still controlled the monetary system. I decided to write this book because as of the date I decided to release this book, no Central Bank or government in the world has presented a single solution that addresses the collapsing global fiat currency system and the burgeoning global monetary crisis in a sustainable and viable manner. Therefore, if we do not take the initiative to implement our own solutions, we will all financially perish, or at a minimum, suffer continued severe banker/government imposed debt enslavement via the monetary system. Hoping someone else will have the courage to implement a solution and remaining silent or inactive is a sure way to sentence all of us to a continued future of misery and financial slavery.

Today, all Central Banks and governments seem only intent on covering up the massive problems in our current monetary system and delaying financial collapse rather than presenting the truth about the system to the public and working towards a viable solution. Without the implementation of a sound monetary system, bankers will retain the power to continually cause cycles of crises in the future. Thus, a sound monetary system is a paramount and NECESSARY first step towards the prevention of massive financial crises in the future. There can be no financial "reform" without the implementation of a sound monetary system and any government or banker that proposes financial "reform" in the absence of establishing a sound monetary system cannot and should not be trusted.

Because Central Bankers and governments currently are colluding in a currency race to the bottom whereby they are

THE GOLDEN GIFT

destroying the purchasing power of all currencies – Pounds, dollars, Euros, Yen, etc – if we, the people, do not stand up, push back and fight for our freedom now, we will soon find ourselves being sold another fairytale after the onset of another banker-engineered global financial crisis of how bankers are going to save us with the creation of another bogus fiat currency like Special Drawing Rights (SDRs) or some other similarly structured monetary product that will be intended to facilitate our enslavement to the bankers even further.

CHAPTER TWO

Ideological Subversion Transforms Lies into Publicly Accepted Truth

Hitler's Chief of Propaganda, Joseph Goebbels, once stated that if an authoritative person told an enormous lie and simply kept repeating it for a long enough period of time through various distribution channels, eventually the majority of the populace would succumb to the lie and start processing the lie as truth. More importantly, due to an enormous vested emotional commitment to this lie that would occur over time, people would also become incapable of processing and comprehending the truth even when it was presented to them. In fact, the inherent egotistical nature of the human mind is so primitive and so strong, that once a lie has been molded in the brain as truth, it will cause people to deny the truth, even when doing so causes them to participate in actions and/or behavior that is detrimental to their own well-being. Thus, once bankers repeated their lies about how our current monetary system operates thousands of times through the institutional academic system, their lies became not only part of our societal folklore but also were gradually accepted over time among the masses as "truth".

Bankers cleverly forged an emotional umbilical cord between their lies and society's belief systems that disallows people from shedding these lies and even from processing the

THE GOLDEN GIFT

truth when they are confronted with it. In a nutshell, this is why the truth about our modern monetary system is so hard to spread to others. Once a young adult becomes convinced that a false principle is true because it has been taught to him for his entire life, it becomes a very difficult proposition to change this belief. This is also why the most well-known former Chairman of the US Federal Reserve, Alan Greenspan, can get away with the lie that "free markets" and "capitalism" were responsible for our current grave global monetary crisis even though not a single one among us has ever experienced a "free market" economy. How can we have free markets today if Central Banks arbitrarily change the interest rates that drive economies? Though any person versed in the simplest and most basic foundations of logic can understand that free markets can't exist as long as Central Bankers are artificially setting interest rates, incredibly most MBA and PhD in economic graduates naively believe that free markets exist today. Because economic professors all over the world teach the lie that our major global markets - stock markets, real estate markets and commodity markets - are governed by free market principles when in fact they are all rigged by the banking cartel, Central Bankers can disseminate repeated lies in the mass media through their puppet representatives that reinforce the belief in these lies among the general masses.

Thus, even when I can invoke historical truths from former bankers, such as those contained in Eccles's 1941 and Hemphill's 1935 statements below, only a handful of people will ever believe them. Today, many economists still confuse the masses with the argument that manipulation of markets can never win. They base this argument on the false claim that even if bankers temporarily prevent free markets from operating, forces of market equilibrium will always quickly return manipulated markets to a free market state. Economists present this false argument on the assumption that nobody would ever accept a negative real rate of return in any capital market. However, this argument crumbles once one realizes that its credibility is based upon the very heavily flawed assumption **that people understand and know real rates of inflation every year.** Instead, the reality is almost the exact opposite. The majority of people in every country in the world believe that "official" government released inflation statistics are accurate, and thus, have no clue as to what are the true rates of inflation.

As an example, let us consider how misunderstanding true rates of inflation can create and support manipulated markets for an extremely long period of time. Today, most global investment firms continue to pitch new clients an annual target rate of return between 6% and 8%. Let's consider inflation statistics produced by Shadowstats.com, a company that produces US inflation statistics using US government formulas utilized decades ago before the US government changed inflation formulas multiple times to deceive the people. Using government-produced and endorsed formulas from decades past, Shadowstats refutes "official" government-suppressed inflation rates and produces REAL inflation rates. For the period 2002 – 2008, Shadowstats concluded that REAL US inflation rates were somewhere between 8% and 12% every single year. Yet, during this very same period, the US government sold its citizens the propaganda statistics of 2% to 4% inflation rates as the "true" rates. Thus, investors that accepted US government propaganda inflation rates and accepted an 8% targeted return from their investment firms during this period accepted negative or zero real rates of return on their investment as their annual target for seven straight

THE GOLDEN GIFT

years. As you can see, we have already disproved economists' assumptions that people would never willingly accept a negative real rate of return.

Furthermore, during this time period, 10-year Treasury notes averaged yields in the range of 3.5% to about 5%. So again, incorporating real rates of inflation of 8% to 12%, 10-year Treasury note holders also gladly accepted negative real rates of return year after year after year. How do I know that they gladly accepted negative real rates of return? Because what person in the world would pour money into an investment if they were informed that the investment would return a guaranteed -7% to -8.5% loss every year? No one. They only invested in these vehicles because they were under the false impression that they were receiving positive real rates of return. The holders of these Treasury notes believed that they were becoming richer because the nominal amount of digital credits that bankers were crediting to their bank accounts was rising. However, because the purchasing power of these digital credits was plummeting, an increased amount of digital credits in one's bank account actually amounted to a real negative rate of return for these investors.

Due to the deliberate dumbing down of society in almost every aspect from academics to music to the arts and media, the majority of people never investigate real rates of inflation for themselves and instead blindly accept the "facts" the banker-propaganda machine feeds them. By simply making every stat fraudulent that people depend upon to calculate real rates of return, it becomes incredibly easy to convince people that markets are free and fair when the reality is that they are 100% rigged and manipulated. And this is how a manipulated market can persist en perpetuity.

Today, we have accounting professors all over the world teaching young impressionable students every day that cash belongs on the asset side of the accounting ledger, when in fact, bankers create all fiat money as debt. It matters not that you can tell someone that believes in the lies taught in Accounting 101 classes all over the world that Marriner Eccles, former Chairman of the US Federal Reserve (1934-1948) stated, *"If there were no debts in our money system, there wouldn't be any money"* (Source: House Committee Hearings on Banking and Currency, September 30, 1941), and that Robert Hemphill, Credit Manager, Federal Reserve Bank of Atlanta stated, *"If all the bank loans were paid, no one could have a bank deposit, and there would not be a dollar of coin or currency in circulation. This is a staggering thought. We are completely dependent on the commercial banks. Someone has to borrow every dollar we have in circulation, cash, or credit. If the banks create ample synthetic money we are prosperous; if not, we starve. We are absolutely without a permanent money system. When one gets a complete grasp of the picture, the tragic absurdity of our hopeless situation is almost incredible -- but there it is."* (Source: Fisher, Irving, *100% Money*, 1935). It is crystal clear from these statements that if money were truly an asset, then of course, it could exist if there were no debts in our system. Banksters have imposed upon us all the use of an entirely fraudulent form of money that is not really money at all. If all people cannot understand the grave fraud of our monetary system given the FACT that the entire global banking system would collapse if all banks called in all their loans, then this is further proof of the fact that the institutional educational system has failed to crystallize people's critical thinking skills properly.

THE GOLDEN GIFT

Furthermore, if all people cannot understand that Central Banks can artificially create a situation of calling in the majority of all commercial bank loans anytime they want by merely raising interest rates to punitive levels, then they will never understand that the alpha bankers at the top of the predatory financial pyramid deliberately and periodically create financial crises for their own monetary gain and to further enslave us through financial ruin. For this reason, I am well-certain that the bankers will unleash another 2008-like style crisis upon the world at some point between 2012 and 2015 and that those that will be the most devastated by this crisis will be those that have not purchased PHYSICAL gold and PHYSICAL silver for protection.

Just as government-released, "official" US and UK unemployment statistics incredulously filter out the unemployed from their unemployment equations to produce false, significantly reduced unemployment numbers today that in no way mirror the reality of the unemployment situation, bankers have filtered out all banking, monetary, and capital markets truth from all academic textbooks over the past century so that billions of people today utterly fail to comprehend the many truths spoken by sound money advocates. Further startling is the fact that much of the fraud of our current banking system was widely known among both politicians and the public a mere 50-70 years ago!

Again, because the aforementioned referenced books, The Road to Serfdom, by FA Hayek and The Theory of Money and Credit, by Ludwig Von Mises, admirably and capably expose all the lies taught about money and our monetary system, I will not spend a lot of time in this book discussing how Central Bankers created a highly immoral and destructive monetary system to specifically enable themselves and large international bankers to create wealth at the expense and misery of all other participants in the system.

Rather, as I stated earlier, I will concentrate on:

(1) explaining why the banking & monetary system is highly immoral and outright criminal; and on
(2) explaining proposed solutions to counter our current immoral monetary system of debt enslavement.

Central Bankers have kept their policy maneuvers secretive for decades and thus, the public-at-large has failed to understand the true roots of real estate market crashes and stock market crashes when they occur. A graduate school professor of mine once stated that Secret Societies like Yale's Skull & Bones are inherently bad and extremely likely to be pursuing dark motives. My former professor stated that if the motives of Secret Societies were honorable, they would not make so much effort to hide their actions from the rest of the world. Due to their lack of transparency, enormous power, and steadfast secrecy, I definitely include the world's Central Banks among these Secret Societies.

One of the primary reasons why people have such a difficult time understanding the immorality of our current banking and monetary system is because people tend to explain concepts they don't understand within the framework they know, even if that framework is based upon lies and deception. Why? It is a well-known fact that immediately following a crisis, whether that crisis is a financial crisis that bankrupts families or a terrorist attack, victims of that crisis desire answers for the triggers of that particular crisis. Victims of a crisis not only seek, but they need, explanations to rationalize the terrible things that have happened to them.

THE GOLDEN GIFT

Thus any explanation, even if that explanation is a lie, is readily accepted by victims to satisfy their need to make sense of a tragedy. As humans, we just don't like uncertainty in our lives and bankers bank upon this psychological phenomenon to manipulate us like puppets. In fact, Naomi Klein wrote an entire book called The Shock Doctrine in which she explains how corporate and banking interests create crises and then exploit the fragile psychology of humans during these crises to build tremendous wealth and to further consolidate their power and control over humanity.

Furthermore, it is much more emotionally comfortable for most of us to continue to accept a huge lie rather than to admit that a concept or idea in which we have believed for our entire lives is actually wrong. Were we to accept a truth that contradicts one of our long-held mistaken beliefs, this admission would then induce in us an emotional state of cognitive dissonance, causing us to experience the disconcerting and uncomfortable feelings of surprise, dread, guilt, anger, and embarrassment. With perhaps the exception of surprise, most people would agree that all of the other emotions are negative ones. Thus, the theory of cognitive dissonance proposes that people have a motivational drive to reduce dissonance by remaining in a state of inertia and denial, even when confronted with overwhelming evidence that their closely held beliefs are wrong. (Source: Festinger, L. A Theory of Cognitive Dissonance, Stanford, CA: Stanford University Press, 1958). This is precisely why so many Jews failed to flee Nazi Germany even when confronted by loved ones that begged them to leave. They didn't want to believe that their way of life was over, and in failing to incorporate the overwhelming evidence that their leaders' morality was rapidly disappearing (as is the case with the morality of bankers today), they refused to relocate, and in essence, sentenced themselves to their own deaths. In fact, as important rights and freedoms have been stripped from citizens in many countries in Europe and in the United States, we are witnessing the same patterns developing today that occurred in Nazi Germany. And unfortunately, today, we are witnessing the same responses as we witnessed in the period that immediately preceded Nazi Germany. Despite the pleas of many for their loved ones to seek safer and more free lands in the face of massive evidence presented to them of the crumbling morality of their countries' leaders, thousands are still incredulously choosing to ignore the massive evidence that their freedoms are ending and are quickly being replaced by a state of tyranny. We can only hope that those that have been warned to take action now but are refusing to do so will awaken from their state of sleep and either:

(1) take action to overthrow our morally bankrupt leaders that are presently consolidating their power across this world; or

(2) execute actions of self-preservation before it becomes too late to do so.

Another reason why billions today fail to accept the truth of our modern monetary system is that many simply choose ignorance over truth due to a delusional belief that if they remain "good little soldiers" to the immoral system, that their loyalty to the leaders of this system will exempt them from persecution in the future. Many people's socio-economic status in this monetary Ponzi scheme is tantamount to the position of a census employee in Nazi Germany. Banking employees whose positions within the banking industry are equivalent to

THE GOLDEN GIFT

census employees under the Third Reich may even realize the grave injustices of the industry for whom they work but believe that their role within this immoral system, such as the role of a bank teller, is one that does not harm anyone because it is far enough removed from the immoral daily machinations of the bankers at the top of the food chain.

Thus, they make a conscious decision to not rock the boat and not to bring potential harm to their current state of well-being within society, believing that as long as they remain faceless within the system, that their survival is a better choice than prosecution that will inevitably come as a consequence of rebellion. A quick risk-reward analysis performed on a cocktail napkin convinces the servants and worker bees of an immoral banking system that remaining acquiescent within the system, even though their lives are becoming harder and less fulfilling, is the better and more acceptable choice than the application of truth to positively change and benefit humanity. They believe that if they partake in the fruit from the Tree of Knowledge, that they will become as naked and vulnerable as Adam and Eve to the wrath of not God, but to the wrath of the banksters. However, this is where their risk-reward analysis bears more holes than a slice of Swiss cheese.

In a highly immoral system that is destined to implode at some point due to the weight of its immorality, no one is immune from prosecution, imprisonment, and even death, not even the workers within the system, except perhaps the top 1% of people running the system. Everyone else firmly sits in the same boat and is fair game for attack and prosecution. Serving an immoral system does not guarantee anyone immunity in the real world game of Survivor. As an example, in Nazi Germany, many people with good hearts and good consciences were unwilling to speak out and unwilling to act, thinking only of their self-preservation, remaining silent and passive, as long as they were not among the group that was currently being targeted by the immoral system. They too made the mistake of believing that passivity was a good strategy to remain anonymous within a putrid, rotten system of immorality.

Martin Niemöller, a German pastor and theologian born in Lippstadt, Germany, in 1892, noted the progression of persecution in Nazi Germany in his now infamous, oft-paraphrased quote below:

First they came for the communists, and I didn't speak out because I wasn't a communist. Then they came for the trade unionists, and I didn't speak out because I wasn't a trade unionist. Then they came for the Jews, and I didn't speak out because I wasn't a Jew. Then they came for me and there was no one left to speak out for me.

Thus, even many of the people that served the Nazi Germany platform and believed that such subservience and obedient silence would keep them safe were eventually imprisoned and killed as the system eventually turned against them. History tells us that knowingly serving a highly immoral system will always end badly for those that lack the intestinal fortitude to extract themselves from the system. I firmly believe that this will turn out to be the case when our highly immoral global fractional reserve banking system implodes at some point within the next decade as well. Those that believe it better to try to disappear into anonymity by dwelling in the faceless bowels of the system will not be safe from those at the top of the system turning against them when the ship goes down. Those that serve as worker bees within the fractional reserve banking system must realize that the great discomfort

THE GOLDEN GIFT

that accompanies the short-term prospects of unemployment will eventually pale in comparison to the totalitarian environment of a total loss of freedoms that will eventually emerge from our current global monetary crisis unless they abandon our current immoral system and help all of us implement a new sound and moral monetary system.

For those of us that dwell on the fringes of the immoral fractional reserve banking system or reside totally outside of it, our choices are not much easier. By accepting the truth about the grave criminality of our modern day banking and financial system, we are forced to reassess and re-think the reasons for almost everything we do - why we go to school, why we work, and why we pay income taxes. In other words, the realization that we spend the majority of our waking hours performing a task just to receive pieces of paper, or more accurately, digital credits in our bank account that can arbitrarily be devalued at will by Central Bankers is certain to evoke very strong emotions, from anger to even helplessness. The necessity of having to change our perception about how the world really operates usually proves to be too daunting for most of us to handle on an emotional and psychological level. Thus, when confronted with a truth as daunting and as altering to our world view as this one undoubtedly is, many of us may choose to respond in the same manner as would an infant. It will not be uncommon for many of us to desire to be left alone, to pound our fists on the table, and to bury our heads in the sand, opting instead for the fairytale that ignorance is bliss. Such reactions may even be natural, as it is our human nature to gravitate towards stability and away from cognitive dissonance.

But, and this is a massive "but" (no pun intended), if we are to even think about freeing our minds from the monetary lies of bankers, the first step we must take to "see" the truth is to become cognizant of the process that was used to taint our belief system. Because most of us remain unaware of the process of ideological subversion that bankers have used for more than a century now to taint our beliefs, we have lived our entire lives never able to break free from the lies of bankers. I literally have witnessed people deny not hypothesis or speculations, but facts about the monetary system, hundreds of times during the course of my lifetime. So what are some of these banking facts that millions of people refuse to accept today? Consider one that I already mentioned above – that money is created as debt and is not 100% an asset. Upon informing people that all paper and digital money is created as debt, I most often receive immediate denials of "that's not true!" or "that's crazy!" even though the deniers are unable to explain the process of money creation themselves. Furthermore, even when I explain the process of how money is created to deniers, and I illustrate to them why no money would exist in the world today if there were no debts, the deniers continue to deny this fact simply because they can not process the revelation that the teachers they trusted taught them lies in school. For those that paid hundreds of thousands of dollars to learn lies in school, they deny this fact even more strongly, as if the fact that they paid $50,000 a year for their education makes it impossible that their accounting and economic professors deliberately told them financial and banking lies and fairytales.

In other words, people deny this fact because they have been told that money is an asset their entire lives, not because they are able to disprove the truth. When people learn that money is created as debt for the first time in their lives, the cognitive dissonance induced by a fact that violently clashes with their belief system short-circuits their neuronal synapses and creates within that person an inability to process the truth, even if that inability is temporary and eventually overcome by intelligence. But for a moment, it is almost as if the neuronal synapses within their brain stop firing and their ability to process facts ceases.

Another of the obvious lies Central Bankers have imbedded in the consciousness of billions of people worldwide is a belief in their stated mission of monetary stabilization. Alarmingly, their goal is the exact opposite – the destabilization of money to prevent the remaining 99.9% of people that reside below them on the socioeconomic pyramid from ever accruing enough wealth to challenge their power. And unfortunately, because the banker's plan of destabilizing all of the world's major currencies – the dollar, the euro, the pound, and the yen – have been so successful, any worker paid in these currencies is severely punished for saving his salary versus opting to immediately spend it.

Today, even when very intelligent people are confronted with the inconvenient truth that a near 98% devaluation of the US dollar since 1913 cannot possibly be aligned with the Central Banker's stated mission of monetary stability, many of them robotically still choose to defend the role of Central Banks in society. And 999 times out of 1000, their defense will solely consist of the regurgitated propaganda that Central Bankers have fed them in classrooms without the injection of a single original or critical thought. People that I've engaged in a debate about the criminal nature of Central Banks have called me foolish to believe that modern economies can flourish without a Central Bank artificially setting interest rates in an economy. They claim that without the existence of what is essentially a criminal Central Bank rigging scheme, economic chaos would ensue. Supporters of Central Banking state this even though a simple, brief historical examination of stable and flourishing economies during periods prior to the widespread existence of Central Banks can easily discredit this piece of propaganda. But such is the process of ideological subversion. A successful ideological subversion campaign banishes facts to the fringe of society while relying on emotion, blind loyalty to authority, and ad hominem attacks (i.e., arguments solely consisting of statements like *"you're a moron", "you're an idiot"* and *"you're a pinhead")* that are absent of any material substance or logic to perpetuate lies. Now of course, some people truly are quite foolish; however, any charge of "moron" should nonetheless not stand on its own but always be accompanied by a logical argument that explains why such a person is a moron.

Central Bankers, through a long, slow and deliberate process, have internalized the lies of our monetary system so deeply within the psyche of the human masses, that it likely will take not just one exposure to the truth, but multiple exposures to the truth through multiple mediums (video, literature, speeches) for the veneer of their numerous lies about our modern monetary system to finally be destroyed. Watch the video called *"How Ideological Subversion of the Retail Investor Enables Financial Fraud"* to understand how Banksters have used psychological warfare over the decades to convince the masses to subscribe to and defend their lies (Please see the References page at the end of this book for the link to this video). Ex-Russian KGB spy Yuri Bezmenov, in explaining the process of ideological subversion, states that it only requires one generation, or about 20 years, for the mass acceptance of a repugnant lie to be accepted as the truth. Why? Bezmenov explained that if trusted teachers taught lies to their students from Kindergarten through the University level,

THE GOLDEN GIFT

eventually this graduating class of young students would marry and become parents. As parents, the indoctrinated young adults would then reinforce the lie by passing it on to their children.

If you are an American or European reading this book, you must realize that you are likely to be more susceptible to banker lies that denigrate the foundations of a sound, honest monetary and banking system, otherwise known as gold and silver. Why? The explanation is actually quite straightforward and simple. Western Central Bankers have been at the forefront of spreading propaganda and lies about our modern banking system. Thus, these lies are most firmly imbedded in the Western education system versus the Eastern education system. I have traveled extensively throughout Asia and the Pacific Rim and can assure you that, generally speaking, it is twice as easy to convince people living in the Eastern hemisphere to convert fiat currency into physical gold and physical silver than it is to convince those living in the Western hemisphere to do the same. Even with Western expats that I meet living in Asia, generally I still find it very difficult to convince them that physical gold and physical silver are a better store of value than fiat currency. In 2008, when I told Europeans living in Asia to convert their Euros into physical gold and physical silver, they told me I was crazy (I stated my belief in converting any fiat currency into gold and my belief that the Euro would face immense problems in future years for the public record in my January 2008 book, Confessions of a Wall Street Insider). Now a mere 4-½ years later, in hindsight, the Euro is in serious trouble just as I predicted and gold continues to be one of the best preservers of wealth, rising about 121% against the Euro from 2008 to mid-2012. If you are a Westerner that has never believed in the merits of gold and silver and the safety that both of these precious metals affords one during a monetary crisis, please take a few minutes to think about the following logic before moving on to the rest of this book.

Whenever the Western banking cartel attacks gold and silver prices in their bogus paper markets that create rapid depressions in gold and silver prices, why have gold and silver prices always recovered all their losses from these attacks for the last 11 years and closed every year higher than it started, with the exception of silver in 2011, when silver suffered slight 8.3% losses against the Euro? Furthermore, why do many Western investors panic during these Western banking cartel attacks on gold and silver prices, executed solely in the fake, banker-controlled paper gold and paper silver markets, and always speak of impending collapses in gold and silver prices, whereas their Asian brethren and sisters consistently use such dips as opportunities to buy more physical gold and physical silver at artificially cheap prices? In fact during one such Western banking cartel engineered decline in gold and silver, as the Western media was falsely spreading news of the end of the gold and silver bull, a friend of mine that visited a gold and silver market in Beijing, China during this exact same period informed me that he witnessed literally thousands of Chinese people buying physical gold and physical silver. Given these bizarrely polar opposite reactions to the exact same event, one must conclude that either there is a genetic trait that Westerners possess that make them more resistant to the idea of purchasing physical gold and silver, OR that those living in the Eastern hemisphere are more willing to purchase gold and silver than their Western brethren and sisters because they have not been subjected to the unrelenting Western banker anti-gold and anti-silver propaganda that is distributed to the masses through the Western media. I will leave you to decide which of these explanations is the more logical and intelligent one.

The unsound nature of today's monetary system, the problem that is the root of all sovereign debt crises and recent sharp plummets in purchasing power of the Euro, the US dollar and other currencies, is directly attributable to Central Banks' unchecked power to create an unlimited supply of money. Central Banks engage in zero central planning that benefits the wealth of their country's citizens, but only engage in central planning that benefits and grows their wealth. Central Banks can create an unlimited supply of money because unlike in the past, when money was backed by gold, today all fiat money is backed by nothing but the "full faith and credit" of a government, which in reality, is a euphemism for "backed by nothing"! Thus all paper money today has as much credibility as Monopoly money. As recently as the end of 2011, I saw a US fund manager argue on a nationally syndicated TV program that dollar denominated US Treasury bonds were a "safe haven". On another popular US TV program, I witnessed another US fund manager argue that gold was a "bad" investment in 2012! When one can essentially buy the same basket of goods with a one-troy-ounce gold coin today as one could during the Roman empire two-thousand years ago, it is hard to understand how someone can argue that dollar-denominated assets that are based upon a fiat currency that has lost 98% of its value in less than 100 years would be "safe", while gold, an asset that has maintained its value for more than 2000 years, would be "bad!

In numerical terms, when the US Federal Government banned private ownership of gold in 1933 and stole US citizens' stores of physical gold in response to a global monetary crisis that the US Federal Reserve and the Bank of

England created, they gave each US citizen USD $20.67 for every one-ounce gold coin they confiscated. At the end of January 2012, that one-ounce 1933 confiscated gold coin that the US Government stole from citizens at a price of USD $20.67 would be worth nearly USD $1,800. On the other hand, the 1933 USD $20.67 the government gave to US citizens would still only be worth USD $20.67 today, and due to massive inflation since then, only be able to purchase a tiny fraction of what USD $20.67 could have purchased in 1933! Knowing that Central Banks all over the world are currently in the process of creating greater rates of inflation worldwide than the inflation rates that existed between 1933 and 2010, if you were given a choice between holding USD $1,800 in cash or a one-ounce gold coin today, which asset would you choose?

Amazingly, I believe from anecdotal stories in which I've asked people this very question, that the vast majority of people would still opt to choose the USD $1,800 in paper money. Again, this illustrates how successful the banker's war of ideological subversion against the people has been. A movie that I really enjoyed recently was a movie called "The Prestige", directed by Christopher Nolan, and starring Hugh Jackman, Christian Bale, Scarlett Johansson and Michael Caine. In this move, Michael Caine's character, Christopher Priest, states:

"Every great magic trick consists of three parts or acts. The first part is called the Pledge. The magician shows you something ordinary: a deck of cards, a bird or a man. He shows you this object. Perhaps he asks you to inspect it to see if it is indeed real, unaltered, normal. But of course...it probably isn't. The second act is called the Turn. The magician

THE GOLDEN GIFT

takes the ordinary something and makes it do something extraordinary. Now you're looking for the secret...but you won't find it, because of course you're not really looking. You don't really want to know. You want to be fooled. But you wouldn't clap yet. Because making something disappear isn't enough; you have to bring it back. That's why every magic trick has a third act, the hardest part, the part we call the Prestige."

Just like every great magician, the global banking cartel has fooled the people about monetary truth for centuries now. "The Pledge" happens when bankers show people a piece of cotton fiat currency such as the USD and tell you that it is "real" money and an asset. Of course, since it is a tangible piece of cloth, this seems like a rational, logical statement but it is not. Bankers introduce all USDs into the world as debt and ONLY a very tiny percentage of all money in circulation exists in the form of paper. Bankers actually create the majority of what we think of as tangible "money" in the form of intangible fictitious digital credits and debits.

It's almost humorous today when people speak of the fact that one day all money will be digital because, though estimates vary due to the secrecy of Central Banks' creation of new fiat currencies during this crisis, it is believed that 98% of the "money" used for all global financial transactions on a daily basis is already digital. Thus, for all intents and purposes, money is already digital. Though your bank account may show that you possess USD $250,000 on your paper statement or on the ATM screen, in reality, your bank only has perhaps 2%, or even less, of this $250,000 in cash in their vaults. If you went to the bank tomorrow and tried to withdraw this as cash unannounced, the bank would very likely be unable to provide you with this money for it would then have to ask its Central Bank to turn your digital money into printed money before handing it over to you. For those that might misinterpret this statement let me explain it to you further. This does not mean that a branch of Bank of America or Citigroup does not have $250,000 of cash in their vaults. Of course they do. What I am saying is that if you took the aggregate amount of ALL deposits from ALL clients at any given branch of any global bank today, they will likely barely have 2% of that aggregate amount in their bank vaults at that given branch, if at all.

The second phase of any good illusion is "the Turn", when magicians make something that was once visible disappear. Bankers execute "the Turn" even better than illusionists because they make the people's money disappear through three separate and distinct channels. Bankers take away the money that people earn through their incomes through (1) the silent mechanism of inflation; (2) a second overt mechanism of the income tax; and (3) initiating capital market crashes. Since most people have no idea that income taxes are a direct transfer of wealth from all citizens in a country to the private banking oligarchs that rule their country, they do not realize that the application of income taxes is a mechanism of theft. Yes, many people are shocked when they learn that income taxes are a direct transfer of wealth and theft by bankers from citizens to themselves, but this is an indisputable fact. If you wish to read the evidence that discloses that nearly 100% of your income taxes go directly into the coffers of the private bankers that run your country, please refer to the findings disclosed by Peter Grace in the Grace Report (Source: J. Peter Grace, The Grace Commission Report for US President Ronald Reagan, January 15, 1984, http://www.uhuh.com/taxstuff/gracecom.htm).

THE GOLDEN GIFT

Bankers execute the third leg of "the Turn" by directly manipulating stock markets and real estate markets to deliberately create stock market and real estate market booms and collapses. When they cause trillions of equity to disappear and when they deliberately collapse stock markets and real estate markets, they know that people will invariably start digging and try to discover the mechanisms by which they *"disappeared"* their money. But all good illusionists will take extreme measures to protect all three phases of their illusion and bankers are no different. Though bankers are always appearing on TV and stating that *"ordinary"* people cannot understand the *"complexity"* of the financial system, this too, is just propaganda disseminated to ensure the success of "the Turn". The motivation of bankers for always promoting propaganda like *"financial derivatives are so complex that even Harvard PhDs have difficulty understanding them"* is simple. Bankers know that if they can convince us that the financial system is much too *"complex"* for us to understand, that we will never start digging for the truth, and thus, never understand "the Turn", the second part of their illusion when they make our money disappear. However, the bankers' argument of *"complexity"* is pure unadulterated rubbish, just as is every other facet of their banking and monetary system. While the mechanisms of financial derivatives may be complex, the mechanisms of fraud are very easy to understand. Bankers funnel our attention to the wrong questions so that we fail to arrive at the right answers.

I can explain the mechanism by which bankers deliberately create artificial *"booms"* and *"busts"* in very simple terms in a couple of paragraphs. When bankers want to create booms, they artificially depress interest rates below interest rate levels that would exist in a free market absent of their persistent meddling. Low interest rates are the proverbial carrot on the stick that banksters use to goad the people into taking out huge loans that they cannot afford. Unfortunately, many of us always pursue the dangling carrot because we unfortunately suffer from a false-sense of confidence that we can game the system to easily earn a much higher rate of return than the interest rate we must pay back to the banksters. However, what most of us don't realize is that the banksters, not us, are in control of this situation as they can call in our loans at any time when they decide it's time to financially ruin us. During the goading phase, our excessive borrowing effectively floods capital markets with money that should not exist and would not exist in a free market and causes a flood of money to chase a limited amount of assets. If, for example, we choose to use this excess money to buy real estate, then the price of real estate soars. Banksters sell this as a *"boom"* in the media to goad even more of us that can't afford loans to borrow more money. In reality, the deliberately created *"boom"* is merely a massive upward and bankster-created distortion and illusion of rising prices that cannot last.

This false sense of confidence originates from a state of euphoria that banksters artificially create through the distribution of massive propaganda in the mass media about endless times of economic prosperity during their manufactured "booms". Compounding this sense of euphoria during times of "booms" is the fact that all agents of the State participate in this scam. For example, let us examine the very public proclamations of the most prominent and revered economists, bankers and politicians immediately prior to the US stock market crash of October 29, 1929 that ushered in a global Great Depression that lasted for more than a decade.

THE GOLDEN GIFT

"We will not have any more crashes in our time." – John Maynard Keynes, 1927.

"There may be a recession in stock prices, but not anything in the nature of a crash." – Irving Fisher, leading U.S. economist, New York Times, September 5, 1929.

"There is no cause to worry. The high tide of prosperity will continue." – Andrew W. Mellon, US Secretary of the Treasury. September 1929.

With ringing endorsements from the most prominent people in the country every year immediately prior to crashes, no wonder so many people every year are goaded into allowing banksters to wipe out all of their capital. And if you think the above was a one time, non-recurring event, merely Google the statements of the US President, US Federal Chairman Ben Bernanke and the most prominent Fortune 500 and Banking leaders in 2006 and 2007, and you will discover that the exact same pattern of propaganda immediately preceded the US housing crash in 2008. In fact, this propaganda pattern is not limited to just these two historical crashes, but they happen everywhere around the world before every single major economic crash. When patterns repeat themselves repeatedly throughout history, if we cannot learn that there is a concerted effort of the State to deliberately scam us, then we deserve the losses that are inflicted upon us when we place undeserved trust in leaders that wish nothing more than to defraud us and lead us into actions of financial ruin. After learning about this pattern of propaganda, either we must accept that the people we have been taught to trust only wish to scam us, or somehow it is a huge coincidence, that all over the world, during dozens of economic crises, we the people, have elected the dumbest politicians possible in our country to a position of power, and they in turn, have made the mistake of appointing the dumbest people in the entire country to the most prominent positions in government and banking. In 1930, even after the US stock market crash had already occurred, there was still no shortage of continuing and relentless propaganda from the government-bankster-corporate machine.

"[1930 will be] a splendid employment year." – U.S. Department of Labor, New Year's Forecast, December 1929.

"I am convinced that through these measures, we have reestablished confidence." – Herbert Hoover, US President, December 1929.

"While the crash only took place six months ago, I am convinced we have now passed through the worst – and with continued unity of effort we shall rapidly recover. There has been no significant bank or industrial failure. That danger, too, is safely behind us."- Herbert Hoover, US President, May 1, 1930.

What we all need to learn from history is that when the banksters decide it's time to pop the bubble and then want to earn money from a real estate market *"bust"* or *"crash"*, as we have since discovered was the exact case with many Wall Street banks in 2008, then there is no stopping them. If and when Central Banks merely decide to raise interest rates and call in loans during times of massively distorted market prices (note that politicians' descriptions of "economic prosperity" is always a lie), they can easily create market panics and crashes.

THE GOLDEN GIFT

Raising interest rates significantly in a capital market causes all excess money to leave capital markets and the prices in that market to then crash. For example in the US, mortgage bankers ensured interest rates on mortgages would rise and cause hardship on people by selling them ARMs (Adjustable Rate Mortgages) during the early 2000s that re-set at much higher interest rates in future years. Mortgage bankers were able to convince people that they would be able to sell their houses for large profits in the rising real estate market environment (at the time) before the ARMs would ever re-set at higher interest rates. Of course, when the real estate market peaked after the bankers had sold millions of ARMs but before the ARMs owners were able to flip their property at huge profits as promised by the banksters, massive numbers of home owners were consequently forced to pay the much more punitive interest rates on their mortgages. In effect, this served the same purpose as banksters calling in their loans. In addition, banksters went wild in the early 2000s selling poor people sub-prime mortgages that they knew the poor would never be able to afford. For example, 90% of sub-prime mortgages that bankers sold to the poor in 2006 were ARMs (Source: Zandi, Mark (2009) Financial Shock. FT Press). Though I am simplifying the description of the process here, I am doing so to demystify the belief in the "complexity" of financial transactions that banksters wish to perpetuate. To create a boom, or more accurately, highly distorted, non free-market prices, banksters merely lower interest rates and coax people into excessive borrowing scenarios. To create a bust, or more accurately, a collapse in highly distorted market prices back to price levels that would exist without banker interference, bankers merely raise interest rates and call in their loans. It's that simple. And the only one making loads of profits from

53

both booms and busts are the banksters. There is also a secondary mechanism whereby banksters can create "busts" in the absence of a rising interest rate environment. In this secondary mechanism, a bust can happen simply due to existing conditions of extreme leverage in capital markets. I'll explain how this mechanism works later in this book.

Finally, we arrive at the third act of the illusion, "the Prestige". The Prestige is the mind-blowing finale that stumps people and leaves their jaws agape. As I stated earlier, whenever a crisis strikes, people have a psychological need to understand the reasons that precipitated a crisis. Since bankers are master manipulators and illusionists, no illusionist ever wants the mechanisms behind his "Turn" to be discovered. Otherwise, magic ceases being magic and the power of the Prestige will die. So when bankers raise the ire of an entire nation by executing "The Turn" and disappearing our wealth, they must necessarily return our "disappeared" wealth to us by executing their final act of their illusion, "the Prestige". "The Prestige" is a necessary act in order to keep the order component of the "New World Order" intact. Execution of "the Prestige" is necessary to pacify the masses and to prevent us from realizing that we are but pawns in a massive global financial scam. This is why we often experience a cycle of rising real estate asset valuations immediately follow a stock market crash and a cycle of rising stock market valuations immediately follow a real estate market crash, *but rarely ever both at the same time.* If you only thought about this fact for a mere minute or so, you would immediately recognize the bankster scam being executed upon us. How can it be that great real-estate market rises often follow stock-market crashes and vice versa? After people have lost great wealth in a stock-market crash is it natural for people to speculate and risk tons

THE GOLDEN GIFT

of their money in another market right away, or do banksters create the conditions that goad people into investing great sums of their wealth into another capital market right away? Hmmmm, I bet you never pondered this question ever before. If the banksters created simultaneous real estate and stock market booms that crashed at the same time, then they would not leave themselves any room to execute "the Prestige". And with no "Prestige", everyone in the world would have already figured out their scam by now.

However, even the execution of "the Prestige" is truly ingenious. Most of us rarely realize that the bankers' execution of the Turn and the Prestige in their worldwide scam relegates us to the proverbial hamster running on the hamster wheel on the fast track to nowhere. Bankers merely return to us through their artificially manufactured "booms" that follow their artificially manufactured "crashes" greater amounts of nominal money that they have already devalued in real terms, thus crippling our ability to gain the necessary financial resources to engineer our freedom from their perpetual tyranny. In other words, the "recovery" part of the boom/bust cycle that banksters sell us is just an illusion and not a recovery at all. In reality, even as we are "recovering" our losses, our "real returns" are still falling. For example, consider that after the banksters crashed the stock market in 2000, you lost $500,000 of your portfolio. After this crash, you swore off investing in the stock market and were lucky enough to ride the Central Bank artificially created real estate price distortion to a gain of $700,000 by 2008 and exited right before the real estate market crash. Well, for most of us, we would feel very good about that. After all, we recouped our entire loss of $500,000 and then made an additional $200,000 of profit, right? Yes, but in nominal terms only. To correctly assess your financial situation, you would have to consider the first phase of the banksters' "Turn", that of inflation. From 2000 to 2008, the US dollar lost approximately 50% of its purchasing power. Thus, $700,000 2008-year dollars only had the same purchasing power of $350,000 2000-year dollars. But recall that you lost $500,000 2000-year dollars. Thus, to recoup your $500,000 of losses in 2000, you would actually have to make $1,000,000 2008-year dollars. But remember, you only made $700,000 2008-year dollars, so even though you ended up with a greater nominal amount of dollars in 2008 than the nominal amount you lost in 2000, you still would have been under-water. The real question is whether or not you would have realized this or not. And that is the beauty of the banksters' "Prestige". They can return money that they stole from us during the "Turn", make us feel good about it, and actually continue to rob us of real wealth at the same time. This is why I repeatedly state that a complete understanding of the fraudulent nature of the global banking system is by far the most important knowledge that you will ever gain in your lifetime. Understand how the game works and you can strip yourself of the many illusions that you have thus far, falsely accepted as truth. But remain ignorant of the banksters' illusions, and you will go to your grave wondering why you felt like a hamster running on a wheel even as your "wealth" continued to grow.

In addition to this grand illusion, bankers' have corrupted our understanding of language to such an extent that most of us still don't understand that when bankers rate an asset as a "Buy", bankers are often selling and when bankers rate an asset as a "Sell", they are often buying. To help you understand banker language more deeply, please Google "The Official Bankster Dictionary and TheUndergroundInvestor." Sadly, when those of us reveal the mechanisms of the bankster

THE GOLDEN GIFT

Pledge, Turn, and Prestige to the public, ad hominem attacks of "that's ludicrous!" have become sufficient enough arguments in our attention-deficit and punch-drunk society to prevent monetary truths from acceptance into the mainstream. Unfortunately, fluff dismissals of the truth that appeal to the emotions of people are particularly effective. As a direct indictment of the shoddy state of our institutional educational system and our media, if a person in a perceived position of authority makes a claim without any supporting evidence, today our mass media is likely to report this claim as the truth with very little, and sometimes absolutely no substantiation at all. In turn, many of us will accept the report as truth without once using our brains to critically challenge such shoddy reporting and journalism and without even realizing that we are being brainwashed.

The massive deterioration of our education system and our media is outlined by a quick investigation into the supremely sensitive topic of how the media is prone to describe military attacks. If one country attacks another, often the "political experts" in the attacked country immediately appear on national TV to inform citizens that their country was attacked because of how much the other country "hates them". Or if two countries have been involved in numerous attacks upon each other for decades, depending on the political alignment of the media and the banker-controlled agenda of the war, one side is often perpetually referred to as "terrorists" while the other side that commits equally as heinous atrocities is always reported as "defending" itself. Always absent in such a discussion is any shred of intelligent analysis regarding the conditions and foreign policies that may have contributed to the hatred that exists between the warring factions, whether such an attack may have been provoked in any manner by one side, or if the "evidence" that the media reports is even true. Though this topic is certainly beyond the scope of this book, I guarantee you that with a little independent research, you will discover that nearly everything the mass media has reported about the conflicts in the Middle East regarding Israel, Iran, Palestine, and the Arab Muslim-Israeli conflict is a lie. If you truly want to form an intelligent opinion regarding this conflict rather than blindly accepting what you have been ordered to believe about it by those creating propaganda that they parade before as real news, I urge you to Google "Israel, Rothschilds, Rockefellers" to learn about these powerful banking families' close monetary ties to the State of Israel, Israel's Supreme Court and Israel's Central Bank. Forget about all the conspiracy, Illuminati articles that this search may return, but rather focus only on the facts and the money trail. If you do so, I guarantee that the facts you will uncover will be shocking enough without the injection of any additional speculation provided by unsubstantiated conspiracy theories. If everything you know about the Arab Muslim-Israel conflict has come from the mass media prior to today, I am sure that the discovery that two powerful banking families are behind the deliberate and artificial creation of this Middle East conflict to serve their monetary and banking goals will be a difficult concept for you to digest. Bankers repeatedly combine fear, hatred, and misdirection as an effective strategy to keep people misinformed, misguided and ignorant about the New World Order that they wish to impose upon us all. It is surprisingly simple to galvanize a nation by invoking strong emotions such as hate by labeling a misunderstood nation as "evil", even in the absence of any hard evidence or facts. Governments, as do bankers, use this technique because they know that emotional appeals, even in the absence of logic and facts, have an

THE GOLDEN GIFT

extremely high success rate in producing their desired response.

As an example of how bankers and their shills continuously ignore facts and use sound bites to shape popular thought, watch the video titled *"Will US Debt Become Junk"* that is listed on our supplemental materials Reference page at the end of this book. In this video, you will see how a financial shill, when confronted with the truth and asked to explain her propaganda, appeals not to a single fact, but only to emotion. With no facts to defend her position, the financial shill resorts to the puerile, unsophisticated yet effective strategy of attacking the person that is trying to expose the truth as *"rude"*. And yet such illogical servants of the Western banking cartel are the personalities that dominate Western media today. As a further example of how emotional appeals are effectively used as weapons by The Powers That Be (TPTB) in concealing the truth, let us investigate the media and newspaper headlines that emerged within the hours that immediately followed the US Oklahoma City bombing of the Alfred P. Murrah building that killed 168 people and injured 680 more on April 19, 1995.

Even though white American Timothy McVeigh was arrested within 90 minutes of the explosion, all initial media coverage for the first several hours immediately following this terrorist attack reported that the explosion was carried out and executed by Muslim terrorists, though there was not a single shred of evidence that existed at the time that anyone of Muslim origin was involved or responsible. If you find this hard to believe, as I stated, perform your own research of microfilm newspaper archives and you will discover this to be the case. Here are just some of the samples of "news" reported in the aftermath of the Oklahoma City bombing.

"The betting here is on Middle East terrorists," stated CBS News' Jim Stewart just hours after the blast (4/19/95).

"The fact that it was such a powerful bomb in Oklahoma City immediately drew investigators to consider deadly parallels that all have roots in the Middle East," ABC's John McWethy proclaimed to Americans the same day.

"It has every single earmark of the Islamic car-bombers of the Middle East," claimed syndicated columnist Georgie Anne Geyer (Chicago Tribune, 4/21/95).

"Whatever we are doing to destroy Mideast terrorism, the chief terrorist threat against Americans, has not been working," declared the New York Times' A.M. Rosenthal (4/21/95).

These are just four examples of the nearly universal US media attempt to immediately sell the 1995 Oklahoma City bombing as a Muslim terrorist act to America without the provision of a single shred of proof. Some moronic *nationally syndicated* American journalists even advocated violence against Muslims in retaliation for the Oklahoma City bombing. This was pandering at its worst to negative emotions of the masses after a terrible tragedy in order to reinforce the manufacturing of news out of thin air. And guess what? As unsophisticated a strategy as this was, elites repeatedly use this strategy because it works and is extremely effective.

Now consider two very important questions regarding the above information. Why did the US media universally blame Muslim terrorists in the immediate aftermath of the Oklahoma

THE GOLDEN GIFT

City bombing without any evidence? For this false belief to be adopted all over the country, whether in New York, Chicago, Los Angeles or Oklahoma City itself, there must have been someone feeding the media the anti-Muslim agenda, who in turn, all-too-willingly nearly cemented these false-beliefs into the psyche of an entire nation. So what or who was behind this propaganda machine? The answer was an "anonymous government source". Time and time again, the American media blindly accepted *"unnamed government sources"* and *"unnamed government officials",* officials that refused to identify themselves and therefore could not be discredited at a later time, at their word, without any credible proof, for having "evidence" that the bombing was executed by a radical Muslim element.

"According to a government source, [the Oklahoma City bombing] has Middle East terrorism written all over it," stated CBS reporter Connie Chung (4/19/95).

Reporter Anthony Mason stated on CBS later that same day: *"Sources tell CBS News that unofficially the FBI is treating this as a Middle East-related incident."*

And the next day, CNN joined the propaganda campaign when Reporter Wolf Blitzer proclaimed, *"It does appear to have, once again, according to an official, the signature of a Middle East kind of car-bombing."* (4/20/94).

The plan to sell to the world that the Oklahoma City bombing was the work of radical Muslims would have worked to perfection had it not been for one small detail. Oklahoma State Trooper Charles J. Hanger stopped and arrested white

American Timothy McVeigh, who later was accused and convicted of the bombing, for driving a vehicle with no license plates, carrying a concealed weapon with no permit, and having no vehicle registration. Though in hindsight, it is easy to identify such flimsy reporting as propaganda, and any intelligent person would likely wonder how he or she swallowed such reported "news" at face value in the absence of any credible evidence, had Timothy McVeigh never been arrested, it is a safe assumption that today, over 300 million Americans would believe the original story about Oklahoma City that someone clearly wanted to sell to America – that Muslim terrorists were responsible for the deaths of 168 and the injuries of 680 more on April 19, 1995 in Oklahoma City.

At this point, you may be asking yourself what in the world does the story of the Oklahoma City bombing have to do with the lies spread by the media about the fractional reserve banking system? The answer, quite simply in one word, is everything. The initial nationwide reporting regarding the Oklahoma City bombing tragedy reflects how the media was complicit in not providing any "news" that day that remotely resembled hard-hitting journalism or even was supported by Journalism 101 basics of fact-checking. Rather, the entire American mass media chose to cater to a government agenda by relying on one unknown anonymous government authority to produce their "news" fear frenzy about Muslim "terrorists" on US soil. In turn, the media's blind reporting of propaganda provided by an unnamed authoritative figure nearly blinded an entire nation from the truth. Recall that earlier, I stated that if one is having difficulty accepting the facts about the fractional reserve banking system I have exposed in this book, one must first understand the mechanisms that can produce such a strong, committed belief in a lie before one is able to see the

THE GOLDEN GIFT

truth. Surely, if one can recognize that an entire nation was one Oklahoma State trooper short of believing a massive lie about the 1995 Oklahoma City bombing based upon a source without a face, then one should be intelligent enough to realize just how easy it would be for bankers to sell lie after lie about the true intent of the banking system to a nation, especially when they put the faces of Hank Paulson, Ben Bernanke, Paul Krugman, Blythe Masters, Bart Chilton, Lloyd Blankfein, Jamie Dimon, Stuart Gulliver and dozens of others of their pawns in front of us.

We have just learned that an illusion is accomplished in three acts - the Pledge, the Turn and the Prestige. We can use this example to also produce an analogy for how the elite have conditioned people to not understand the truths about our monetary system and our current global monetary crisis. The elite have often mixed ideology with lies during the Pledge phase to gain widespread acceptance of their lies, used the Turn phase to introduce vulnerability and doubt, and finally used the Prestige phase to cement society's belief in their lies. Thus, the elite have determined that it is not even necessary for them to alter reality to control people but that it is only necessary for them to alter our *perception of reality* in order to control us and prevent us from challenging their power. If we can understand that reality is always a constant but that our *perception of reality* has been altered, then we will take a very large step forward in understanding the root causes of our global financial and monetary crisis. The most important thing anyone of us can do to free ourselves from the mental shackles banksters have imposed upon us is to start closing the massive gap that banksters have created in the financial and monetary industry between *the fantasy of our perceived reality and the truth of actual reality.*

The power of this concept is why former Goldman Sachs CEO and then US Secretary Treasury Hank Paulson always focused on the importance of restoring market confidence during the first phase of the global monetary crisis in 2008, yet never once addressed the root of the problem - the immoral fractional reserve banking system. Paulson knew that if he could alter our perception of the problem, then we would then passively allow the problem to persist. For example, when Hank Paulson needed to convince US Congress of the necessity of massive socialist bailout programs for US banks that would have undoubtedly gone bankrupt without this assistance, he repeatedly and deliberately referred to the **"restoration of market confidence",** not to the restoration of sound money principles, the restoration of a sound banking system, or the restoration of economic stability.

"This troubled asset relief program [for US Banks] has to be properly designed for immediate implementation and be sufficiently large to have maximum impact and restore market confidence." – Hank Paulson.

It was not Hank Paulson's prerogative to fix a broken, immoral system, but he desired merely to bolster our confidence in a broken system and to alter our perception regarding an inherently immoral broken monetary system. Of course, these immoral bankers, including Ben Bernanke, blitzed the mass media with a mountain of bogus stories about a recovering economy and "green shoots" that temporarily did fake out a very naïve public and bolster our confidence that banksters could "fix" the economy. However, since the bankers' Modus Operandus was simply to alter our perception of reality without ever actually altering our reality, here we

THE GOLDEN GIFT

stand in 2012, once again on the verge of economic & financial Armageddon. It has always been the elite's goal to subdue us into passive and unquestioning acceptance of their orders and commands through changing our perception of reality. Thus, they use the institutional education system to convince us of the merits of their system even as they continue to "dumb us down". They spread their rule of lawlessness through the land by convincing us that their immoral laws are keeping us safe even as their goals are to implement more and more draconian rules that are designed with only one goal in mind - to protect their moneyed interests from the rest of us. Though these last two points are beyond the scope of this book, let me touch on these two points briefly. If I can convince you that these two points are indeed true, then you will much more easily understand the other critical points of this book. Though there is a mountain of historical evidence that substantiates and confirms that the Rockefellers' and Carnegies' purpose in developing a standardized global curricula of education was to produce obedient servants for the Industrial Revolution (please refer to the sources quoted in the References page at the end of this book), one can easily prove that critical thinking and intelligence is not an aim of the educational system through a simple exercise of anecdotal observation.

How many people do you know that consistently engage in Hero Worship and that stubbornly defend the honor (or dishonor as is the case in many instances) of a famous personality without ever having spent a single day, hour, minute or even second in their presence? If you are like me, then you know many people that fit this bill. In this regard, I'm not talking about the defense of clearly moral people like His Holiness Tenzin Gyatso, Burmese spiritual leader Aung Sang

Suu Kyii, and Mahatma Ghandi. I'm merely speaking of the adamant defense of very public figures like athletes, rock or pop stars, celebrities, and Presidents and Prime Ministers, of whom we know very little other than their publicly created image. Obviously, we all know that famous people have press agents and public relations people that paint a public image of this person that can significantly differ from their private image and private personality. Tiger Woods is a prime example of someone whose very marketable and public "good guy" image was destroyed by the realization of his real personality.

Yet, time and time again, I've heard people defend Presidents, pop stars, and celebrities with the same vigor and possibly even more fervor than they would defend an immediate family member, even though such behavior defies all sensibilities and logic. Perhaps if people paused for even a minute to think about their furious defense of iconic personalities, they would realize that they know nothing of their idol's morality and true character, having never spent a single moment with this person. So what is the explanation for a person's seemingly unbendable devotion to a celebrity such as Eminem, President Obama, PM David Cameron, or Michael Jordan without the benefit of any interaction with said celebrity?

This illogical devotion to an idol is a direct product of a person's inability to think for themselves and of their inability to distinguish between the fantasy of perceived reality and the truth of actual reality. And what is responsible for this form of mental illness? In my opinion, it is the educational system's deliberate failure to foster critical thinking. If education really cultivated people's critical thinking skills, there would be almost nobody in our society that engages in Hero Worship.

THE GOLDEN GIFT

However, since education is designed to cultivate obedience to authoritative figures, and famous personalities hold a definite level of authority in society, many people blindly assign good "star" qualities to famous people without any critical evaluation of that person. Assuming a famous, prominent person is a person to be admired without truly knowing the first thing about them is tantamount to a situation in which every stranger you met believed that you were a wonderful person and endlessly heaped praise upon you even though they knew nothing about you. If you would think such behavior to be odd and illogical were you the recipient of such adulation, then certainly you should find the blind adulation of Presidents, Prime Ministers, athletes and celebrities equally as puzzling and odd. But because most of us never ponder such scenarios, we never realize that the elite have designed the education system to present us with the "perception" of education while in fact, it achieves the exact opposite – the systematic stripping away of our critical thinking skills and the implementation of principles of obedience and compliance to authority. In fact, any object of idol worship, were he truly a moral woman or man, would urge people not to worship him or her, as blind worship of a man or woman actually encourages such a person to act immorally rather than morally. This is exactly why Buddha stated the following:

"Don't blindly believe what I say. Don't believe me because others convince you of my words. Don't believe anything you see, read, or hear from others, whether of authority, religious teachers or texts. Don't rely on logic alone, nor speculation. Don't infer or be deceived by appearances...Do not give up your authority and follow blindly the will of others. This way will lead to only delusion...Find out for yourself what is truth,

what is real. Discover that there are virtuous things and there are non-virtuous things. Once you have discovered for yourself give up the bad and embrace the good."

Unfortunately, most of us do the exact opposite of what Buddha urged us to do. We blindly believe everything anyone in a position of authority orders us to believe. If we didn't, there wouldn't be millions of misinformed people filled with anger and hatred as a result of their misunderstanding of military conflicts and terrorism today. We are constantly deceived by appearances. If we weren't, we would consistently accept as truths, lies presented as news in the absence of any factual evidence. And lastly we almost never find out for ourselves what is truth and what is real. If we did, then our entire global banking system would not exist today, as it can only exist with the acquiescence of billions.

As far as the legal system, an investigation of the unjust application of either tax laws or drug laws should easily convince you that the legal system is much more about protecting the ability of the elite to maintain their power and protecting their moneyed interests versus regulating morality and preventing immoral acts. Many more deaths are reported worldwide from "legal" prescription drugs like Vicotin, Oxycontin, Xanax, Paxil, Wellbutrin and Valium than from all the deaths attributed to heroin, cocaine, crystal methamphetamine, and marijuana combined. Among the reasons that many more people die from "legal" drugs than "illegal" drugs are the failure of regulatory agencies to prevent pharmaceutical companies from marketing their drugs to unintended users like teenagers and the failure of regulatory agencies to ensure that pharmaceutical companies properly disclose dangerous potential and serious side-effects of their

drugs like suicidal thoughts, the onset of psychoses, the potential of birth defects, and the induction of heart palpitations. Yet the never-ending "War on Drugs" has never seriously targeted the half-a-trillion dollar a year pharmaceutical industry for their role in spreading death because legislators are funded by the industry and are consequently much more concerned about protecting the moneyed-interests of the industry than in protecting us from their immoral marketing tactics. (Source: Gutierrez, David 2008. Prescription Drugs Kill 300% More than Illegal Drugs, Retrieved June 10, 2012 from *the Truthout* website: http://archive.truthout.org/111208HA and Smith, Andreas Whittam, 2012. GlaxoSmithKline – And You Thought the Culture at Barclays Was Sick, Retrieved July 3, 2012 from *The Independent* website:
http://www.independent.co.uk/opinion/commentators/andreas-whittam-smith/andreas-whittam-smith-glaxosmithkline--and-you-thought-the-culture-at-barclays-was-sick-7912502.html).
With their passage of many laws, the elite are not concerned with the reality of a situation but only concerned about altering how reality is perceived and in convincing people that something is "wrong" or something is "right" despite the fact that the public perception of this particular topic may be entirely wrong.

One must realize that tyranny or evil does not have to be in your face or drastically obvious for it to exist and for it to greatly influence your beliefs and your life in a highly negative manner. In fact, the elite would prefer that their tactics remain unknown to most. It is much better for them to gain control over us and to keep us passive by controlling our perception of reality rather than attempting to alter our reality in a manner that would be offensive to our humanity and sensibilities. If the elite have a choice between presenting an offensive reality that consolidates their power or altering our perception of reality so that we remain calm and subservient, they will choose the latter option 100 times out of a hundred. I remain convinced that the first step to freeing ourselves from the tyranny of banksters is to bridge the gap between our perceived and actual realities when it comes to the global banking and monetary system. As banksters have repeatedly exploited this gap time and time again to mislead and misguide us into executing investment behavior that is not only unfavorable but also harmful to our best interests, it is self-evident that this gap is still quite considerable. If we recognized that such a gap existed, we would not allow ourselves to be repeatedly fooled by the same tactics day after day, month after month, and year after year. Thus, the first goal of every single person reading this book should be to tear down the curtain of the financial Wizard of Oz.

THE GOLDEN GIFT

CHAPTER THREE
The Gold Standard Ain't Broken And It Never Has Been Broken

The half-life of uranium isotope 238 is about 4 billion years. The half-life of a US dollar in recent times, has been about 8 to 10 years. With the half-lives of all paper currencies becoming shorter and shorter, there is no doubt that the timeline for paper currencies reaching their intrinsic value of zero is increasingly being expedited. In fact, the time that financial panic will descend quickly and forever negatively alter the landscape of our current global financial system may be a reality that is a lot closer at this current point in time than most people are willing to accept. I firmly believe that taking significant positions in precious metals (specifically physical silver and physical gold) BEFORE the panic arrives is the only thing that can save one from the banker-instigated wealth destruction hysteria that will inevitably come and I do believe that we will experience this financial ELE (Extinction Level Event) that kills all fiat currencies in our lifetime. Again, the only people that view this possibility as "crazy talk" are people that do not understand monetary truth. Every single fiat currency in the history of the world has eventually ended up collapsing. This is an indisputable fact. Every single fiat currency in the history of the world, from fiat currencies used during the ancient times of Chinese dynasties to the fiat currency used in modern day Zimbabwe, have all collapsed due to the very same reason –

the surrender, in that Empire or Nation, of the power to inflate and deflate currencies at will to bankers.

History has taught us that when such a power is given to a small concentrated number of people in a nation, that the people given this power will never use this power to produce economic stability, but only use it to transfer the nation's wealth to themselves and to control all people below them. In fact, history has taught us that people given such a great power will always eventually use this power to remove the very ability of that nation to function as an ongoing viable economic entity and eventually trigger its utter economic downfall. Einstein once stated that it was insanity to do the same thing repeatedly but yet expect a different result from the next repetitive action. Yet, though we have thousands of years of history to draw upon from which it is self-evident that money backed by nothing will always collapse and that granting monopolies on monetary creation always leads to tyranny, we seem not to be able to learn from prior tragedies and continue to yield despotic power to Central Banks and continue to accept fake immoral money as our primary means of conducting trade today.

For those of us that use the thousands of years of monetary history to extrapolate present day conclusions from past day events, we know that it is absolutely insane NOT to expect the US dollar, the Euro, and the Yen to eventually implode and collapse as long as we allow them to be backed by nothing. So if we know from history that our current monetary system collapse is not a matter of if, but when, the only determination that remains is whether it will happen in our lifetimes, or the lifetimes of our children or our grandchildren. Though the argument regarding the timeframe of when we should expect an utter collapse of our current fraudulent monetary system is

THE GOLDEN GIFT

beyond the scope of this book, not to mention the fact that it is near impossible to pinpoint a precise date when this will happen, it is of my opinion that if one studies the signs that preceded all other collapses of fiat currencies throughout history, the current signs indicate that utter collapse of our current fiat currency system is coming soon and that it will happen not during some generation 100 years from now, but that it is poised to happened during OUR CURRENT GENERATION.

Of the people that understand the necessity of owning physical gold and silver (and not the GLD and SLV ETF which will provide no security when the second phase of the monetary crisis commences), many still erroneously believe that returning to a gold standard or a bi-metal gold/silver standard is a futile proposition. Many people believe that if the bankers remain in control of a gold-backed currency that they would continue to manipulate currencies for their own benefit. If bankers only care about controlling the monetary supply, and if they continue to do so, gold-backed or not, why would a gold-backed currency help us? These are all fair and useful questions in helping us to determine WHY the arguments against the reinstatement of a gold standard hold no merit. So let's examine the claims of gold standard failures in past history, and in the process, expose more banker lies and propaganda.

Many academics around the world have given false legs to banker propaganda by helping forward the very false notion that there have been periods in world history where a gold standard failed to control runaway inflation. Thus, bankers state, if a gold standard cannot prevent the most destructive force against economic growth and production today, high inflation, why should we ever consider returning to such a system? Others that bemoan the current fraudulent state of banking today, academics among them as well, also incredulously support the false notion that a gold standard is "unworkable". This particular anti-gold standard faction falsely argue that as long as a corrupt criminal element controls a gold-backed monetary system, then these criminal elements will eventually corrupt even an honest system into one that they use for criminal means, and thus, there is no reason to even attempt to implement an honest sound monetary system. This anti-gold standard faction argues that one has to purge the criminal element from lording over the banking system first or it matters not if a sound or unsound monetary system exists. As long as a criminal element controls the monetary system, this faction argues, the criminal element could lie to us and not even implement a gold standard even if they tell us they are doing so, right?

In this next section, I aim to explain why both these arguments against the re-implementation of a gold standard are without merit. It is important to note that in all historical instances when a gold standard supposedly "failed" to prevent significant inflation, inflation was ushered in by a Central Bank's decision to ABANDON the gold standard and not due to a failure of the gold standard itself. Claiming that the gold standard failed to uphold monetary value during a period in which bankers abandoned the gold standard is akin to a situation in which a pregnant woman sues the manufacturer of birth control pills because she became pregnant AFTER she stopped taking the pills. Furthermore, those that argue that we must purge the criminals that operate our criminal banking system today from the banking industry before a gold-backed monetary system would ever honestly operate have never considered that if we purged the criminal elements of the

THE GOLDEN GIFT

criminal banking system first, then criminals would have no incentive to remain imbedded in the industry and would voluntarily quit the industry. For example, when Prohibition laws were overturned and manufacturing alcohol was once again legalized, the ability of criminals to make millions from illegally shipping and distributing alcohol disappeared and the criminals disappeared from the alcohol industry. Likewise, if you removed the criminality of the monetary and banking process, the ability of banker criminals to illicitly make billions of easy profits would disappear and the criminals would then disappear from the banking industry.

Furthermore, to be crystal clear that a gold standard has never failed to admirably perform its job of enforcing price stability and to prevent conditions of runaway inflation, let's examine the oft-given example of Bretton Woods. Critics, or more aptly put, disingenuous banking shills like Paul Krugman, state that gold standards simply do not work. They falsely state that Bretton Woods failed to prevent runaway inflation and thus serves as sufficient proof that any subsequent attempt to implement a gold standard in the future would also fail again. However, during Bretton Woods, the US Central Bank never implemented a true gold standard in which gold reserves backed a constant percentage of every US dollar they elected to create. In other words, the US Federal Reserve secretly created a large quantity of US dollars backed by nothing (essentially our current day system), even though they falsely informed the world that they were creating dollars backed by gold. In the process, they secretly diluted the gold standard and did not maintain a gold standard. Had the US Federal Reserve actually maintained a true gold standard, inflation would have been kept at a very low rate. The decision of the US Federal Reserve to deceive the world and to refuse to maintain the gold standard is the act that ultimately led to the collapse of the Bretton Woods agreement. So at this point and time, many of you may be thinking, *"Haven't you just proven the argument that as long as the people in charge of the banking system are corrupt, a gold-backed currency will not protect the people?"*

ABSOLUTELY NOT. AND HERE'S WHY.

Even though Bretton Woods was a pseudo, and not a true, gold standard, it still protected the holder of US dollars against banker fraud a million times better than today's unsound monetary system that bestows Central Bankers with the unchecked power to create an unlimited supply of new money as debt and to create money that is backed by nothing. The event that caused the owners of the US Federal Reserve to lobby President Nixon and then under-secretary to the US Treasury, Paul Volcker, to end the gold standard, was France's demand of gold bullion from the US Federal Reserve in exchange for its significant supply of trade-surplus US dollars. France knew that the US Federal Reserve had failed to honor its pledge of maintaining a true gold standard and that the US Federal Reserve was creating millions of new dollars backed by nothing to fund an intensifying Vietnam War. So they called the bankers' bluff and demanded gold in return for their supply of paper dollars – paper dollars that were being debased by the American Central Bank's failure to maintain a true gold standard. The private families that owned the Central Bank feared that they would lose valuable gold and receive significantly devalued US dollars in return (due to their scam of not maintaining the gold standard). Consequently, Nixon's advisers, including Volcker, ordered President Nixon to slam the door shut on the gold standard when Great Britain followed France's lead and demanded to redeem $3B in devaluing US dollars in gold (Source: Packard, Kathleen, 2011. Was Nixon's Treasury Official Right to Worry About Going Off the Gold Standard? Retrieved May 10, 2012 from *the Business Insider* website: http://articles.businessinsider.com/2011-08-23/markets/30089787_1_convertibility-paul-volcker-trading-partners).

Up until the gold standard ended, even though it was not a fully honorable one, it still performed its job of protecting US dollar holders. When the Central Bankers tried to enact fraud under the standard, they lost something valuable (gold) and in return received devaluing assets (paper dollars) they did not want. And this pattern would have continued indefinitely until either:

(1) The bankers decided to honestly reinstate the gold standard again, thus stopping the incentive of nations to convert their USD into gold, or

(2) They lost all of their gold and were left with worthless dollars.

Thus one can see that as long as the gold standard was maintained, it would have performed its job in protecting the holders of money versus protecting the criminals that destroyed the gold standard. The only way that the criminals could protect themselves was to end the gold standard. Thus since neither of the two above options were palatable or appealing to the bankers, the only real decision for bankers of their above two options was to END the gold standard. So once they ended the gold standard, the banker criminals could continue perpetrating their fraud against the people. However, if the gold standard was maintained, their continued perpetration of fraud would have been impossible.

But the end of the Bretton Woods agreement was not without important lessons. We learned that the gold standard, when corrupted by immoral bankers, provided a mechanism for the people to protect the valuation of their money. This is precisely what a gold standard is designed to do. It doesn't matter if bankers do not maintain a true gold standard because a gold standard allows the people to punish the bankers for this fraud once they uncover it. Had the gold standard been maintained, every country in the world that maintained a large US dollar surplus would have been able to punish the owners of the US Federal Reserve System for their deliberate and secret debasement of the US dollar and their simultaneous abandonment of the gold standard. The gold standard unequivocally did not fail to uphold US dollar valuation under Bretton Woods. The bankers unequivocally failed to uphold the gold standard and this is why so many economic problems consequently ensued. **However, banker historians have reversed cause and effect and have re-written history books to advance their lie that it was not the bankers' dishonesty that created economic problems during this period, but that it was the implementation of the gold standard.** And today, banker pawns like Paul Krugman advance these lies.

If one attempts to use a sophist argument that Paul Krugman is a Nobel Prize winning economist so therefore he must know best when he states that a return to the gold standard is, in his own words, *"crazy"* idea for nut jobs only, then again, one has fallen victim to not using his or her brain to

THE GOLDEN GIFT

separate fantasy from fact. One should realize, before assigning any credibility to these various awards, that the Nobel Peace Prize committee awarded their "prestigious" award to one of the most war-enamored Presidents in US history, Barack Hussein Obama.

As another example in history of when the gold standard performed its job of protecting the people's wealth that predates the one above, let's consider the history of money in Great Britain during WWI. During WWI, the banking families that controlled the Bank of England also failed to maintain the gold standard much as the Federal Reserve failed to maintain the gold standard pre-1973. Consequently, when the BoE created massive supplies of British Pounds backed by nothing in order to fund Great Britain's participation in the war, they increased Great Britain's money supply from roughly $5 billion pre-war to roughly $12 billion post-war. Though the bankers destroyed the gold standard in Great Britain in order to fund the war, after the end of the war, they refused to revalue severely debased post-WWI British pounds at lesser amounts of gold. Instead, the Bank of England tried to sell the lie that they had not violated the gold standard and maintained the pre-war British Pound-to-gold conversion ratio. When people realized they were being duped by the banksters, they started to exchange their British pounds for physical gold in massive quantities, again returning highly devalued paper money to the bankers and receiving much more valuable gold in return. Eventually, to stop the loss of gold from their coffers, the Bank of England eventually shut down the gold standard.

Thus, the gold standard never failed to uphold the value of the US dollar during Bretton Woods and never failed to uphold the value of the British Pound during WWI. Rather, the US dollar and the British Pound lost great value due to the failure of bankers to uphold the gold standard and their attempt to cheat citizens of their wealth with devalued money that went off the gold standard. Inflation soared because bankers abandoned the gold standard and NOT due to the gold standard as banking shills falsely claim. As such, these examples, though referred to by bankers today as prime examples of failures of the gold standard, hardly can be labeled as such. Rather they are just examples of the lack of banker morality. If bankers created new money during wartime, as long as they backed the creation of every single new note with the same percent of gold as existing notes (as is supposed to be the case under a gold standard), then paper money would not have lost huge amounts of its purchasing power during these times. Again, it is the bankers' abandonment of the gold standard in history that caused massive inflation, not any failure of the gold standard itself. Furthermore, one has to understand that nearly everyone used to understand how money worked during the historical periods when sound money existed, unlike today. Therefore, whenever a government desired to go to war with another government, the citizens of both warring nations understood that a resultant war would likely mean that gold standards would be abandoned and their money would be devalued. Thus, during historical reigns of sound money, the constant state of an informed majority was opposition to war, unlike the perpetual war-mongering of many citizens today that ignorantly and astoundingly *celebrate their own wealth destruction because they have zero understanding of monetary systems.* The equivalent of a citizen's professed pride in their country bombing another country back to the stone age would be if that person witnessed robbers cleaning out his house and did nothing but not cheer them on and help them carry out his possessions. The idiocy of applauding a country's war efforts abroad when there is no direct threat of invasion from the attacked country is mind-boggling because this cheerleading is applauding a very significant theft of one's wealth and savings. Consequently, a sound money system, because it encourages diplomacy over war, would undoubtedly significantly reduce the number of active wars and theater engagements around the world. Perhaps, due to the trillion dollar profitability of the military-industrial complex, this is why gangster bankers have the full support of the military-industrial complex in upholding an immoral, unsound monetary system today. Greed and profit are very strong motivators to the continuation of extremely immoral behavior and systems.

In addition, when we examine history, even if a country temporarily abandoned the gold standard during war, as long as it re-implemented it after the end of war, the debased currency in question rapidly regained its lost purchasing power. Post Civil-War America is a perfect example of this. If one merely looks at the chart presented in the article titled *"The Rise & Fall of the US Dollar (1800 to 2009)"*, by Sean Malone, that I've included in the Reference section at the end of this book, the correlation between a return to a gold standard post-Civil War and the rapid re-valuation of the US dollar from a highly devalued state is clearly apparent. In fact, these historical occurrences once again illustrate the effectiveness of the gold standard in protecting citizens' wealth against the fraudulent schemes and great proclivity of bankers to cheat and steal wealth from its citizens.

I also would like to add one final note about the gold standard during WWI Great Britain and during the Bretton Woods system (1944-1971). Both these gold standards functioned under fractional reserve systems of banking. As I will explain later in this book, for a true gold standard and a true sound monetary system to operate, the system of fractional reserve banking must necessarily be destroyed. If one understands this, as I hope all of you will by the time you finish reading this book, then you should understand the following: the fact that the gold standard of Great Britain and of Bretton Woods was still able to admirably protect the value of money for citizens for a long duration under what was arguably much less than optimal conditions only serves to strengthen the argument today for the introduction of a 100% backed gold-monetary system today.

Finally, let us conclude this examination of the merits of a gold-backed monetary system by investigating the topic of war. Keynesian-educated bankers like Paul Krugman, along with the banker-owned mass media, often not only describe war as "good for the economy" due to the massive amounts of new money that Central Banks create during war that they falsely argue provides "economic stimulus", but they also openly lobby for war even during times when no apparent enemy exists. In fact, Paul Krugman incredulously wrote an Op-Ed piece in the New York Times in which he voiced support for a government creation of a "fake alien" invasion due to the subsequent resultant job creation in the defense industry that he believed would end the US's economic woes. However, using wars, fake or real, to provide economic stimulus and as a "wealth creation" tool is about the farthest possible reality from truth.

If you understand the above historical examples I have provided in which war created massive currency devaluation and a much worse standard of living for the vast majority of citizens that were living in the countries that had engaged in war, then you should be able to see through the immorality of banking shill Paul Krugman's argument. Any new money that

THE GOLDEN GIFT

is created out of thin air during war steals massive purchasing power and real wealth from the savings of all citizens that reside in the countries that wage war as well as all worldwide holders of those currencies. Stimulus created by war is a false stimulus and the only true profiteers in this equation are Central Bankers and those corporations directly involved in wartime efforts such as weapons manufacturers and defense contractors. That is why you should also realize that the Nobel prize has become a joke and is often awarded not to people that forward peace prospects and humanitarian efforts but to some of the biggest misanthropes in the world that forward the agenda of states and criminal bankers.

Under our current system, bankers continue to punish the people with their fraudulent manipulations of real estate markets, stock markets, FX markets and commodity markets, and we the people, currently possess no mechanism to fight back within the false financial matrix that bankers have created for us other than to buy physical gold and physical silver. This is why re-establishing sound money through a gold standard or a bi-metal gold & silver standard will be the only way to restore our freedom and to correct everything that is wrong and criminal with capital markets and currency today. It is very important for you to understand that our current banking system is not only immoral but that it is downright criminal. If you would not allow me to bring a Glock 17 firearm into your home, point it at your head, and demand at a minimum, that you hand me 30% of your earnings every year, then you should not be "fine" with what bankers are doing to your wealth today. In essence, they are committing the exact same crime against you every year, using their abilities to manipulate interest rates and manipulate capital markets instead of a Glock 17 firearm to commit these crimes. The only difference between these two situations, and I do mean the ONLY difference, is that the mechanism by which an armed robbery nets criminals ill-gotten gains is fully understand by the general public whereby the banking-created mechanisms that nets banksters the EXACT SAME ILL-GOTTEN GAINS are not understood by the general public. If you would protect yourself from the first type of theft by shooting any home invader that attempts to strong-arm you out of your hard-earned income, then you truly need to ask yourself why you are not actively doing everything in your power right now to oust and imprison the bankers that steal substantial quantities of your wealth from you every single year.

Owning gold and silver is a hedge against this fraud, but exercised in isolation among few people, such a strategy does not afford everyone protection against bankster fraud. However, if we can convince enough people to convert the majority, or even 10% of their fiat money savings, into physical gold and physical silver and hold their savings in the form of precious metals, then private ownership of gold and silver would collapse our fraudulent monetary system and pave the way for a new sound monetary system. I explain the mechanisms for how mass ownership of physical gold and physical silver, even in small quantities and low participation rates, would trigger the collapse of monetary fraud and pave the way for a new financial renaissance in my companion book, <u>The Bankers' Secret Plot to Bankrupt the World & How We Can Stop Them!</u>

In any event, common citizens such as you and I do have the opportunity to free ourselves of the immoral shackles that banksters have placed upon all of us. For the first time in decades, bankers are beginning to lose their grip on their price suppression schemes against gold and silver. Unfortunately, as I've pointed out earlier in this book, this immoral cartel of bankers continually conjures up new fraudulent schemes (i.e. the gold and silver ETFs, the GLD and SLV) to replace their old failing ones. As existing literature and facts about the GLD and SLV ETFs point to very likely massive fraud, one would be very wise to avoid these two ETFs at all costs (again, please refer to the Reference list at the end of this book for articles that explain why this is the case).

Hopefully, by now you have realized that bankers are relentless when it comes to the execution of fraud upon the people. There is no lie that a banker will not tell to a client to defraud him or her, even the lie of informing a client that the bank is buying allocated physical gold and physical silver on his or her behalf when he or she is not actually doing so. I highly recommend that you never buy any physical gold or physical silver from a bank and allow a bank to store it for you. One day you may just discover that you hold only air. As a last ditch act of true desperation, I have even heard banking shills try to convince people that a gold standard would severely limit the growth of global economies when in fact a return to a gold-backed monetary system would likely create the strongest period of stable economic growth the world has ever witnessed. Because gold itself is a rare metal and there is a limited supply of it, banking shills have tried to convince the people that a gold-backed monetary system would be dangerous because it would act as a bottleneck on economic growth. This may be true under an unsound monetary system like the one we have today but under a sound monetary system, this would never be a concern. Let me explain. Many people today still believe the lie that the reserve ratio requirement is 10% and that the US banking system can only create $10 million worth of loans from a $1 million deposit due to the fact that viral movies like Zeitgeist have popularized this myth and US finance professors in the US still teach this lie in classrooms. However, one only needs to read my article *"An Exploration of Madoff's $50 Billion Ponzi Scheme Will Unveil the Root Causes of this Global Monetary Crisis"* (contained in the list of articles and videos in the Reference page) to source the facts that disprove this lie. The truth is that today, the US banking system can create up to nearly $100 million of new money out of thin air for every $1 million of deposits. Thus, if one tried to implement a gold standard to back our current criminal and fraudulent monetary system, then of course that would be a crazy concept. But the whole purpose of reinstating a gold standard is to free citizens from the conditions of financial slavery imposed by bankers upon us by our current system. Before we could implement a gold-backed monetary system that would create massive economic growth, many aspects of our current banking system would first have to necessarily be demolished and reconstructed.

Imagine if my business made $100,000 not in profits, but in revenues in one year and that I immediately flipped and leveraged this money to create $10,000,000 worth of financial products from my $100,000 in revenues? Then, if I created enormous wealth for myself from these products, I would keep all of the profits to myself. However, if I lost the entire $10,000,000 because I made insane, sociopathic, utterly irresponsible risky bets with that money on unsound financial propositions and then plunged $9,900,000 into debt because of imaginary money that I created that should never have existed in the first place, imagine that I could ask someone to re-create for me an additional $9,900,000 out of thin air and be re-capitalized every single time such an event would happen?

THE GOLDEN GIFT

Think about how furious everyone would be at me? But this is essentially how the banking system operates today. If you don't understand this analogy, then you must realize that you understand very little about how the banking system operates today. Bankers have no accountability whatsoever for creating fake money out of thin air and then using this fake money to try to maximize profits for themselves only. On the rare occasion their extremely risky bets pay off, they keep all the profits with no benefit whatsoever to the vast majority of their clients. And this insanely immoral and unsound structure to our monetary system is the first thing that would have to be destroyed before one could implement a sound gold-backed monetary system.

The first thing we would need to do in order to implement a gold standard is to scrap the idea of fractional reserve banking. Under a sound system, bankers would never be able to clear $500 million in 10 years for themselves, as did many Wall Street CEOs in the 2000s, but would actually have to engage in moral, productive behavior to earn their money. And this is precisely why bankers so adamantly attack and belittle the viability of a gold standard. If we were to return to a gold standard and sound money system, the sewer dwellers of morality such as Lloyd Blankfein, Jamie Dimon, Vikram Pandit, and Brian Moynihan would become obsolete dinosaurs and be washed into the stink hole that they themselves created. The great irony of our fraudulent monetary system today is that the fraud is so widely misunderstood that I doubt that even the children of the aforementioned banking executives realize the grave criminality of their own parents. The role of a bank under a sound monetary system should simply be to facilitate the flow of money in an economy for the exchange of goods and services and to earn nominal fees for the delivery of this service, period. The role of banks should unequivocally not be to use other people's money to make risky bets to earn money solely for themselves. Think about this concept. With no other industry in the world do shareholders accept such an illegitimate role in society except with the banking industry.

Imagine if Steve Jobs, when he was still alive, used Apple's $100 billion cash reserve to invest in risky Credit Default Swaps in the EU and then subsequently lost all $100 billion. Steve Jobs would undoubtedly be ousted as CEO at the very next shareholder's meeting. However, when bank CEOs engage in the exact same behavior with the exact same results, the CEOs of these banks reward themselves with huge multi-million dollar and euro bonuses to supplement their enormous multi-million dollar and euro salaries. Even in the event that an alpha-bankster's irresponsible behavior causes his or her company to go bankrupt and in the process destroys the lives of thousands of his or her employees, these banksters still reward themselves with obscene golden parachutes even as they flee their sinking ships. As an example of this never ending corruption, even though Merrill Lynch went belly up, lost more than $8 billion during their last year, and was assessed an $8.4 million fine for securities fraud in 2007, then CEO Stan O' Neill awarded himself with a $48MM windfall during his last year of employment and took another $159MM in severance when he led his company into bankruptcy. And though the government easily could have stopped this insanity, the government decided that it had no problem with O' Neill pillaging and plundering US citizens' wealth through his bank (Source: Clark, Andrew, 2007. Merrill Lynch, the firm lost $8B and the chief executive had to go – with $159MM. Retrieved May 10, 2012 from *the Guardian* website: http://www.guardian.co.uk/business/2007/oct/30/6). The role

THE GOLDEN GIFT

of a bank, as it is today, should never be to make risky bets with other people's money whereby all clients are burdened by the losses and receive no benefit from the gains. A business by any name other than a bank would be prosecuted for racketeering under the US Federal RICO *(*Racketeer Influenced and Corrupt Organizations) Act.

For a sound monetary system to be implemented, two steps are required. First, all banks should be required to maintain a 100% reserve ratio requirement at all times, and never be allowed to multiply this money with "magic" money creation as is the case today. In other words, we should kill the concept of fractional reserve banking forever. If we were to implement this first step, then our current money supply would likely be contracted by hundreds of times. Central Banks today create a great amount of money within our banking system to fund bankers' fraudulent price distortions in real estate markets, commodity markets, and stock markets so that bankers can create wealth for themselves at the expense of the public that do not understand these price distortion mechanisms. Thus, if we instituted a sound monetary system, the amount of money we would need to fund the stable, organic economic growth of nations would greatly decrease, and the amount of gold that would be needed to back all currency under a sound system would also shrink exponentially. Recall that I mentioned that "busts" in the boom/bust cycle can happen in the absence of significantly rising interest rates simply due to the concept of leverage. In very simple terms, when banks can create $10MM, $50MM or $100MM of loans from a customer's $1MM deposit, this exemplifies the concept of leverage. When you require all banks to maintain a 100% reserve ratio requirement, however, you remove the risk of leverage from the economy and allow the economy to experience steady, stable organic growth versus the artificial creation of wildly unstable economic cycles that result in massive price distortions to the upside and eventual steep crashes to the downside.

The argument that fractional reserve banking is necessary to fund economic growth is a specious argument used by bankers to support their current immoral system that allows them to effortlessly transfer wealth from the masses to themselves. Fractional reserve banking always leads to devaluation of fiat currency values. By extension, bankers that argue for the continuation of fractional reserve banking also argue, as idiotic as this may sound, that the devaluation of savings and a loss of wealth is a necessary condition for economic growth. Even a third-grader educated to think for himself or herself could poke holes in such an absurd, ludicrous argument. Banksters are the ones that benefit the most from a fractional reserve banking system to the detriment of 99.9% of citizens that inhabit this planet, and that is why they have always argued that their immoral fractional reserve system is "necessary". This is why the continue to plant specious arguments that a gold-backed monetary system would constrict economic growth in textbooks and in New York times best selling books like <u>The Lords of Finance</u>.

Thank God that there are plenty of authors and students of our current monetary system that have already thoroughly discredited the need of a monetary system to allow banks to create money out of thin air as a pre-requisite for economic growth to occur. To this end, I highly recommend Chapter 3, Legal Attempts to Justify Fractional Reserve Banking, of Jesús Huerta de Soto's book <u>Money, Bank Credit, and Economic Cycles</u> for further disclosure of why the adoption of a fractional reserve banking system to spur economic growth is a

THE GOLDEN GIFT

specious argument. And if you need more proof of the illegitimacy of our current fractional reserve banking and monetary system, please perform your own research and you will discover that the major religions of Islam, Hinduism, Judaism and Christianity all issue harsh warnings against usury and condemn usury as a certain way to enslave people. You will also discover that many ancient thinkers of note throughout history, including Plato, Aristotle, Cicero, Seneca and Plutarch, have condemned usury as a surefire way to undermine and destroy the integrity of nations (as well as others whom I have quoted in this book). Among more modern-day great thinkers that all identified credit expansion, usury, and fractional reserve banking principles as the origin of economic evils were Thomas Jefferson, Thomas Randolph, Daniel Raymond, Senator Condy Raguet, John Adams, US Congressman Louis McFadden and Peter Paul de Grand. Yet incredibly, due to the public's lack of understanding of this issue, usury, today, is a built-in mechanism of fractional reserve banking that people accept as easily and as willingly as the fact that the sky is blue!

For those that may believe that the abolition of fractional reserve banking is uncharted territory and that we have no historical precedent for knowing whether or not an alternate system would work, please allow me to present the operational history of the Municipal Bank of Amsterdam. The Municipal Bank of Amsterdam, established in 1609, actually maintained a 100% reserve ratio with respect to all demand deposit accounts for nearly 50 years and maintained a near 100% reserve ratio for more than 150 years. After 36 years of operation, by 1645, the Bank of Amsterdam's deposits grew to 11.28MM florins (the currency in Holland) with 11.8MM in reserves. Due to the fees the bank earned from the execution of money safekeeping duties and for facilitating other financial transactions, reserves actually grew to more than 100% of deposits, a feat that would be impossible by today's flimsy immoral fractional-reserve banking standards. Of course, the Bank of Amsterdam's fee schedule was vastly different than banking fee schedules today, with their fees of a very nominal, not exorbitant, nature, and only enough to offset operational costs and to produce nominal profits or no profits at all as opposed to the excessive immoral banking fees of today that gouge customers to produce huge profits for banks. Imagine that? Sound banking led to banks that were almost non-profit in nature. Economic growth in Amsterdam was steady despite the Bank of Amsterdam's unwillingness to create money out of thin air to stimulate economic growth, further disproving modern banksters' arguments that a sound monetary system would serve as a bottleneck to economic growth rates. This situation of a general state of equilibrium between deposits and reserves existed *for more than one hundred years* up until 1722, when both deposits and reserves grew to about 28MM to 29MM florins.

Furthermore, even when the credit-expansionist French banking system that occupied Holland created incessant worries of massive inflation and consequent bank runs in 1672, only one bank, the Bank of Amsterdam, maintained the ability to effortlessly return all deposits to all customers that wished to withdraw their money from the banking system. Though one may gasp in surprise at the notion that a bank was able to return as much money as any client wanted during a time of financial panic, under an honest banking system, ALL banks would ALWAYS be capable of returning 100% of all deposits to 100% of all depositors at all times without any problems. The Bank of Amsterdam eventually lost its prominence and

THE GOLDEN GIFT

power only when the City of Amsterdam demanded that the bank make massive loans to cover the growing costs of the Anglo-Dutch war in the 1780s. This action forced the Bank of Amsterdam to drastically and tragically cut its reserve ratios from 100% to 25%, and when news that they had been allowing some customers to withdraw more than 100% of their receipts became public knowledge, the 170-year run of sound banking and sound money at the Bank of Amsterdam came to an end. Despite this tragic end, the fact that the Bank of Amsterdam and the City of Amsterdam were both able to flourish under sound monetary principles in direct contradiction to today's fraudulent monetary teachings and arguments from Ivy League scholars and professors amply demonstrates the benefit of sound money. (Source: Huerta de Soto, Jesús. 1998, Money, Bank Credit, and Economic Cycles, pp. 98-105).

As a final addendum to buttress the campaign for the feasibility and applicability of a sound monetary system, let me deconstruct the final complaint banker shills use to scare the public out of wanting a return to a global gold-backed monetary system – the so-called impossibly high price of gold that would be necessary to do so. I often like to expose false arguments by posing a question in response, as often the best way to expose false arguments is to compel critical thought. That said, let me present to you the following question. How can it be a crazy proposition for gold to rise to $20,000 an ounce (the sometimes quoted necessary price of gold to return to a gold-backed monetary system), while it is simultaneously sane to allow bankers to continually create massive amounts of more new fiat money and devalue it on the road to zero? The answer, of course, is that a price of $20,000 an ounce gold is not crazy if such a price really were necessary and that it is not sane to allow continual devaluation of fiat currencies. Already, the US Federal Reserve has devalued the dollar to such a degree that a 2012 dollar is only worth two to three cents of the value of a 1913 dollar, the year the Feds started their criminal operations. Yet we are still led to believe that allowing Central Banks to create money continually out of thin air is not only logical but GOOD FOR THE ECONOMY whereas a $20,000 an ounce price of gold is insane.

A high quality, flawless 3 carat diamond can easily run in the neighborhood of USD $50,000 to USD $100,000 or higher. In March 2012, diamond dealers around the world quoted the price for a one carat flawless diamond as somewhere between £11,450/$18,000 and £26,000/$40,872.
(Source: http://www.18carat.co.uk/onecaratdiamond.html and http://www.diamondse.info/)

One troy ounce is roughly the equivalent of 155.51738 metric carats as both are units of weight. Thus, in regard to diamonds, one troy ounce of diamonds is already priced somewhere in the ballpark of USD $2,790,000 to USD $6,3500,000. Today, the vast majority of people accept that paying $2.8MM to $6.4MM per troy ounce of diamonds is a "normal and sane" price to get married, but these very same people believe that paying USD $20,000 for a troy ounce of gold is "crazy". The only reason this situation exists is because bankers have fed us propaganda for decades that have instructed us to believe that insanely high prices for diamonds and absurdly low prices for gold are "normal".

For centuries, we have accepted banker propaganda as truth without ever using the grey matter inside our skulls called our brains. The pathetic fact is, most of humanity has ceased questioning banker propaganda today and has blindly and unthinkingly accepted the whole stinking pile of rubbish as truth. There is no compelling reason to believe that gold at even $20,000 an ounce is a crazy price if such a price were necessary to establish a gold standard once again. Should not a precious metal that can help possibly solve our global monetary crisis and possibly save hundreds of millions of people from starvation be valued at a minimum of USD $20,000 a troy ounce? Is not a metal that can help solve poverty and terrorism worth at least USD $20,000 a troy ounce? Even though I would answer these questions affirmatively, allow me to deconstruct banker propaganda even further. The figure of gold at $20,000 an ounce is one that has been based upon the estimated supply of US dollars in existence during this current decade. With the US Federal Reserve creating trillions more dollars out of thin air every year in response to this crisis, perhaps this $20,000 an ounce figure is now even low. Still, the estimate of $20,000 an ounce is based upon a gold standard currently applied *to our current unsound monetary system.*

As I've already explained above, before a gold standard can be implemented, we must incorporate other massive changes in our current banking policies, such as banning the practice of fractional reserve banking. Since our current system is so fraudulent, it only makes sense that scrapping our current system and starting over from scratch would be necessary to implement a sound monetary system. Why would just backing fraudulent money with gold within the confines of a fraudulent monetary system help solve our current monetary woes? The answer, of course, is that it would not. Thus, scrapping our current banking system and imposing debt forgiveness worldwide would be the necessary first step towards implementing a sound monetary system. Of course, such a step, I presume, would receive massive opposition from the top

2% of banking executives in the world as this would mean the collapse of their banks and the end of their tens of millions of annual dollar and euro salaries. However, given that the majority of debt that clients of banks have accrued over the past several decades was immorally imposed upon us due to the nature of our current monetary system that creates all money as debt, I would 100% support the forgiveness of nearly all bank-related debt. In fact, I would say that massive debt forgiveness of all bank-related debt would be the only moral choice if we wish to establish sound money ever again. If banking executives argue that debt forgiveness is an excessively punitive punishment for their century long period of transgressions against us, then I have a simple solution to their complaint. Let us calculate all the bank theft during our entire lifetime through their immorally imposed inflation, social security taxes, income taxes, rigging of Libor interest rates, rigging of stock markets, and their rigging of gold, silver, oil and all commodity markets. Let us take them to court before a jury of our peers, not their peers, and let us determine the damages the bank owes us for stealing portions of our wealth for our entire lifetimes. Then, with the proceeds of these settlements, we will gladly pay back our collective debts to them. Since debt forgiveness would cost the banks just a fraction of my hugely fair and just alternative solution of debt forgiveness, the banks should opt for debt forgiveness. If banks opted for debt forgiveness as part of the solution to establishing sound money, then we could very significantly contract the current monetary supply to just a fraction of its current amount and thus be able to set the initial price of gold in a gold-backed sound monetary system at a much lesser conversion rate than USD $20,000 per troy ounce.

THE GOLDEN GIFT

Debt forgiveness should be enforced as a prerequisite to institute a sound monetary system for all of us as the global banking cartel has already reaped trillions of dollars of undeserved and ill-gotten gains from illegitimately creating money as debt instead of creating it as a pure asset as it would be under a sound, moral banking and monetary system. The greatest obstacle to overcome today in instituting a sound monetary system is simply one of education and knowledge of the truth. The fact is that no one alive today has grown up in an era of honest banking. Thus, the bankers have been able to convince us through academia and education that usury, theft, and the use of our deposits to simultaneously enrich themselves and destroy our wealth is a "fair and honest" system. Stop reading for just five minutes to digest that statement. If you ponder the implications of that statement, you will realize that you have not lived one free day in your entire life, a mind-boggling realization. Once people understand the travesty of our current immoral system, it will literally be impossible for the banksters to keep imposing this system upon us.

The Bank of Amsterdam, for the first 50 years of its operation, was a model for how a legitimate, honest bank within a sound monetary system should operate. In this model, the bank made virtually no loans, engaged in no risky deals, and only charged fees for its money-storage and transaction services, the profits of which were more than adequate to pay the salaries of its bank officers and managers. In other words, banking employees and executives, in a system where a bank functions to facilitate sustainable, steady economic growth, would give up their undeserved titles as the wealthiest members of society and earn very modest income levels only. In turn, they would once again regain their respected status among society as one of the greatest pillars, instead of one of the greatest villains, of society. Once all of us understand that a gold standard could most assuredly work and serve as the backbone for a sound monetary and banking system, so many of the other immoral absurdities of our current criminal system will become abundantly and crystal clear.

For example, in the United States today, a US government agency, the Federal Deposit Insurance Corporation, otherwise better known to Americans as the FDIC, guarantees the safety of deposits in member banks, up to $250,000 per depositor per bank as of January 2012. The absurdity of this "safety net" which gives many American participants of the US banking system a very false sense of security, is that as of December 31, 2011, according to the FDIC's own data, the FDIC fund contained a piddling $9.2 billion to insure $6.979 trillion of deposits. The FDIC reserve fund constituted, as of the start of 2012, a mere 0.13% of all insured deposits in the US banking system. Now remember that all banks in the US do not have FDIC insurance, so if you include all deposits within the US banking system, the FDIC fund covers an even ridiculously lower percentage than 0.13% of all deposits. So what does this mean in plain English for any American or any holder of US dollar-denominated financial products of any nationality? Basically, the FDIC pledge means nothing, and if a large US bank like Bank of America or Citigroup were to fail, there is no possible way that the FDIC could insure and return depositors' accounts without having to drastically devalue all US dollars in existence. In other words, because all the money in the FDIC fund would disappear in a New York minute during a bank run, the FDIC would have to ask the US Central Bank to create more money out of thin air just to return to the failed bank's depositors, the money that the bank owes them in

THE GOLDEN GIFT

the first place. Thus, the US Federal Reserve would necessarily have to greatly devalue and counterfeit the existing US dollar supply and impose a silent tax on every single US dollar in existence just to return the money to US depositors in the event of a bank failure.

If you understand what I just explained to you, one should realize that there literally is no insurance on any deposits in any bank in the US no matter what the banksters try to tell us, and that the current sorry state of the FDIC fund provides not insurance, but rather a *guaranteed theft of your wealth if a bank failure occurs.* Great insurance plan, huh? But this is exactly the fraudulent mechanisms by which the criminal banking system provides insurance. A similar analogy would be the following. Consider a situation in which you were robbed and then called the police. Upon arrival, the police then informed you that if they were lucky enough to recover your stolen goods, you would have to pay them a 30% recovery fee to re-obtain your goods. This is exactly why every single citizen right now should be willing to fight their politicians and to fight their bankers to return our great nations to an honest and moral banking system. Nobody wins under our current banking system except the top 0.01% of this world.

JS KIM

CHAPTER FOUR
Fully Understand Monetary Debasement to Know How to Protect Yourself During this Monetary Crisis

Understanding the concept of monetary debasement and the criminal act of usury that accompanies monetary debasement as an everyday practice of global bankers today is crucial to understanding why our current monetary system is so fragile, unsound, and responsible for much of the world's most urgent problems today. No suggested financial reform will ever have any benefit to us unless it includes a gold standard or a bi-metal gold/silver standard. The founders of America understood with great clarity the need for a sound monetary system to be established, maintained and upheld and for a material to be used as money that would present limitations upon its creation and present difficulties to counterfeit it as a precursor to conditions of liberty for all citizens. Paper and digital money, our "modern" money, fit neither of these qualifications for sound money. In fact, the founding fathers of the US ensured that any person found guilty of debasing newly coined American money would suffer death. Furthermore, the founders of America wrote provisions into the Coinage Act of 1792 that disallowed paper money backed by nothing to ever be used or accepted as a form of money. The founders of America understood the need for a sound money system that did not allow for unlimited credit expansion and they not only feared, but they also knew that such a system would eventually

THE GOLDEN GIFT

lead to financial enslavement of the masses. Below, I have presented the exact language contained in Section 19 of the US Coinage Act of 1792 that first established gold and silver coins as money in the newly formed Republic of America.

"And be it further enacted, That if any of the gold or silver coins which shall be struck or coined at the said mint shall be debased or made worse as to the proportion of fine gold or fine silver therein contained, or shall be of less weight or value than the same ought to be pursuant to the directions of this act, through the default or with the connivance of any of the officers of persons who shall be employed at the said mint, for the purpose of profit or gain, or otherwise with a fraudulent intent, and if any of the said officers or persons shall embezzle any of the metals which shall at any time be committed to their charge for the purpose of being coined, or any of the coins which shall be struck or coined at the said mint, every such officer or person who shall commit any or either of the said offences, **shall be deemed guilty of felony, and shall suffer death.**"

Today, as I've explained numerous times within this book, scoundrels that leverage our current monetary system of felony reward themselves with unbridled and unspeakable riches committing the very act that the founding fathers of the Republic of America said should be punishable by death. In fact, every Central Bank and every commercial bank in the world commits the very felony that our founding fathers explicitly stated should be punishable by death. We really need to understand how banksters have successfully gained widespread acceptance of a monetary system so heinous and despicable that those that fought for freedom stated the penalty for its implementation must be death. The first US Treasury Secretary, Alexander Hamilton, was the author of the 1792 Coinage Act. Hamilton was instrumental in helping the House of Rothschilds European banking family establish the new Republic's first and second Central Banks. Consequently, some historians have speculated that Hamilton was a Rothschild agent and that the reason for the harsh death penalty of the 1792 Coinage Act may not have been to protect the citizens of America. These historians have speculated that perhaps the Rothschilds instituted the death penalty for devaluing America's money as a means to grant the First Bank of the United States absolute control over the valuation of money. However, I disagree with this line of reasoning and argue that while Hamilton may have been manipulated by the Rothschilds into establishing the First and Second Bank of the United States, he still remained a staunch defender of sound money principles and liberty.

In any regard, this point of contention regarding Hamilton's allegiances does not negate the fact that sound money incapable of being arbitrarily devalued is inseparable from the concept of personal freedom. Today, if we wish to regain an incorruptible freedom in the future, we must once again return the crime of deliberately debasing money to the status of a felony punishable by death. Today, Central Bankers and commercial banks have remained free to flourish in their criminal felonies of debasing every single fiat currency in existence and harming the wealth of billions all over the world. This criminal act grants bankers a nearly risk-free mechanism to build their wealth while virtually performing no work and expending no effort. If one states that this cannot be true because of the collapse of Wall Street titans Bear Stearns, Lehman Brothers and Merrill Lynch in 2008, one has to realize

THE GOLDEN GIFT

that I am speaking of risk-free to the bankers only. Remember I informed you that Stan O' Neill cleared about $207 million in salary and severance during the year Merrill Lynch failed because his bank assumed too much risk. Obviously, there was no risk of Stan O' Neill losing any wealth from any of his idiotic and immoral decisions. Only Merrill's employees and Merrill's clients lost an enormous amount of wealth from the bank's risky business behavior and practices.

It should be simple to understand why bankers have engaged in such a foul-spirited propaganda campaign to ensure misunderstanding of this mechanism. Not only do academics bash the gold standard as an implausible solution to our current monetary crisis although their arguments are patently wrong, but brainwashed civilians amazingly also partake in this propaganda campaign alongside the banksters. The root of civilians' misunderstanding of our current global economic problems almost certainly is the institutional academic system. In numerous instances, young adults' beliefs have been led astray by leading academics that dispense propaganda on behalf of bankers. Internationally recognized awards such as the Nobel Prize in economics are virtually meaningless today as such awards elevate the authority and visibility of certain economists that bankers have hand-picked and funded to disseminate their propaganda to the rest of the world. In fact regarding the curricula of business schools today, there are so many lies taught as truth, that a business education, in my opinion, needs to be re-branded as a "miseducation". I for one, 100% believe that a business education outside of Austrian economics, whether at the undergraduate, MBA, or PhD level, constitutes an act of pissing one's money down the toilet.

Because there have been so many banker myths propagated over centuries that gold is a "useless" metal with no value, I would like to devote a portion of this book to a discussion of why gold and silver still unequivocally provide the basis for a return to a sound monetary system. I believe that those that believe that gold is a barbarous relic because it *"just sits there"* and because *"you can't eat it"* are falling victims to the da Vinci criticism that *"anyone who conducts an argument by appealing to authority is not using his intelligence; he is just using his memory."* If one merely thinks about these two criticisms of gold that have been sold to the world by Warren Buffet and then parroted by millions of others, these arguments are simple to deconstruct after a very short period of introspection and logic. Using this same argument, one would have to conclude that diamonds, rubies, pearls, sapphire, emeralds, jade, etc. all have zero intrinsic value and should all be free of charge. Although diamonds are one of the hardest substances in the world and thus have lots of uses for drilling and cutting, synthetic diamonds today can also serve this same role. The primary purpose of real diamonds today is still exclusively as jewelry that "just sits there". To those that accept the argument that gold has no use because "it just sits there", then one would have to dismiss the possibility that any semi-precious or precious stone has any intrinsic value as well. However, somehow I find it impossible to believe that not one of the sheeple that parrots Warren Buffet's argument against gold, if they are married, has ever bought a diamond engagement ring.

Buffet's argument that gold *"has no use"* is incredibly naïve, incredibly stupid, and incredibly deceptive because gold's best use is its oldest use – its use as money. There are many reasons that gold and not rubies, pearls, or diamonds, has been widely used as money for thousands of years. If diamonds possessed the monetary properties of gold, then

THE GOLDEN GIFT

history would be full of ancient and modern cultures using diamonds, not gold, as money. In fact, gold also has wonderful conductivity properties and would be the standard metal used in many electronic products today were it not so rare. The only reason gold is only used in high-end electronic products is because its rarity causes its price to be too expensive for common conductivity use. Believing the various aforementioned banker-spread lies is as naïve as believing that US and European stock markets haven't been tremendously manipulated by bankers and governments every year since the overt onset of our global financial crisis in 2008. As one of the most difficult properties in maintaining a lie is the fact that one must always create a new lie to cover for an old lie, at one point, the liars always slip up, refute one another, and mistakenly expose the truth of their bastardly money system.

For example, Warren Buffet takes every chance he gets to publicly denigrate gold as a "useless" metal. Yet, when US Federal Reserve Chairman Ben Bernanke was questioned by US Senator Ron Paul on July 13, 2011 in the US House Financial Services Committee meeting as to whether or not gold was money, Bernanke, in his attempt to refute the belief that gold is money, slipped, and replied that gold is not money but only a "precious metal." But how can it be "precious" when Warren Buffet states that it is "useless"? Furthermore, if Bernanke desires to define money not by its value but by its intrinsic make-up, then he should define dollars not as money but as "cotton cloth." In the classic detective movie sequence in which two suspects are questioned separately and then their answers cross-examined, such directly contradicting answers to the same question would be interpreted to reveal that one of the two suspects, Buffet or Bernanke, was caught in a bold-faced lie. Obviously an asset that is "useless" cannot simultaneously by "precious". If we accept Bernanke's word that gold is "precious" but not "money", then we should ask Bernanke why exactly does the US Federal Reserve hold gold? What "precious" role does gold serve to the US Federal Reserve? If gold is not money and only "precious" jewelry, is the US Federal Reserve interested in holding jewelry as an asset? And if the answer to this question is yes, why does the Fed not opt to sell all of its gold for diamonds? After all, I just explained to you earlier that diamonds, according to its price per troy ounce, are 1,500 to 4,000 times more valuable than gold as of May 2012. Why does the US Federal Reserve not hold diamonds in their vaults if gold is not money? Certainly the equivalent monetary value of diamonds would require less storage area than gold. Or is it possible, since the same private banking families that control the US Federal Reserve, the Bank of England and the European Central Bank also control the world's diamond cartels, that they refuse to hold diamonds because they already know that the prices they set for diamonds are 100% fraudulent? Obviously, one can easily see that due to these frequent slip-ups of Central Bankers and their cronies, it is quite easy to poke huge holes in the voluminous propaganda they teach and promote about fiat money, gold and silver. If you wish to understand more fully the myths about gold and silver spread by banksters yourself, please view the two videos labeled "gold myths" in the Reference page at the end of this book.

In conclusion, there are plenty of viable and sustainable solutions to our global monetary crisis that exist, just none proposed by bankers or politicians at the upper echelons of our society. Bankers, and in particular western Central Bankers, vehemently and violently oppose all sustainable solutions to our dire global monetary crisis. If sustainable solutions were

THE GOLDEN GIFT

implemented, starting with a sound monetary system, then western Central Bankers would lose the power to artificially inflate and deflate asset prices at will, and thus lose their economic control over the nearly 7 billion people in this world.

CHAPTER FIVE
The Solution Must Come From the People

In today's age, technology has made many of us lazy and given us a false sense of entitlement. Instead of believing that we can change the world, we wait for governments and bankers to do this for us. Throughout history, this is a platform for positive change that has NEVER worked. The achievement of any significant positive change has always occurred through the work of individuals, not governments.

Motivated governments gravitate towards bureaucracy and stagnation, upholding the status quo and eventually evolving towards tyranny. Motivated, positive individuals gravitate towards creativity, progress, activism, and freedom.

Mahatma Ghandi led the movement that freed India from British colonial rule, not the Indian government. Nelson Mandela inspired the movement that eradicated Apartheid, not the South African government. Malcolm X and Martin Luther King Jr. inspired the oppressed in America to fight for and to win Civil Rights liberties and to help eradicate the domestic terrorist group The Ku Klux Klan, not the US government. We must rely on the work of individuals, not governments, for change. Any government that has made the promise of change has never executed this promise successfully. Both the Vicente Fox government in Mexico as well as the Barack Obama

THE GOLDEN GIFT

government in America rose to power on great emotions of the masses that believed their false promises of change, yet neither President delivered any real positive change to the people regarding our current economic and monetary system. Promises of change are normally the platforms of politicians that desire to win elections but rarely desire to implement real change. **Elected government and appointed banking officials, because it is in their best interest to maintain the corrupt social paradigm that exists, will ALWAYS oppose any type of positive change that benefits the majority of people in their countries.** If one understands how the political system really works, one will understand that those with the most money in a country always select powerful politicians and then merely make it look as if they were elected. Powerful elites present an illusion of choice that the masses gobble up and digest all too quickly without a second of critical thought or analysis that would reveal the truth.

Consider the Malaysian state of Kelantan's announcement in August, 2010 that they would accept Islamic Gold Dinars and Silver Dirhams as an alternate currency. In response to this announcement, an extremely positive development to protect the wealth of the people, the Malaysian Central Bank promptly declared the use of gold and silver money as illegal within 24-hours. All Malaysians should have seen the Malaysian Central Bank's proclamation as utterly hypocritical as they declared Islamic money as illegal within a predominantly Muslim country. The Malaysian Central Banker actions clearly demonstrate the immorality of the banking interests that control Malaysia. Even though immoral Malaysian bankers (most likely controlled by Western interests) continue to fight Kelantan's use of gold and silver as real money, for now, the moral, honorable people of Malaysia are winning this battle against corrupt, immoral bankers. In fact, by August 2011, just one year after Kelantan made this positive development the law, the gold dinar had already appreciated against the Malaysian Ringgit by 30% while the silver dirham had appreciated against the Malaysian Ringgit by an astounding 100%. This is the power of real money. Furthermore, the Kelantan introduction of the Gold Dinar and Silver Dirham as money clearly delineated the fight between good individuals and corrupt governments.

Menteri Besar Datuk Nik Abdul Aziz Nik Mat, a key figure in implementing gold and silver as money in Kelantan and the executive director of the state-owned Kelantan Gold Trade Sdn Bhd mint, described the circulation of gold and silver as a *"great, great moment"*. In contrast, because this moment has threatened corrupt Malaysian bankers and politicians' mechanisms for creating easy wealth for themselves, they have viewed this moment as a terrible, terrible moment. Kelantan Economic Planning, Finance and Welfare Committee chairman Datuk Husam Musa said gold and silver would not be recognized as currency within Malaysia and the Central Bank of Malaysia declared the ringgit (RM) as the only legal tender in the country. The battle in Malaysia regarding the people's right to use gold and silver as currency clearly illustrates that corrupt bankers will abandon their religious teachings in a heartbeat when these teachings threaten their greed and their corruption. Still, Kelantan to this date, has ignored their government declarations and have embraced the use of gold and silver as money within their state.

The struggle in Kelantan between the good of the people and the immorality of government interests that want to crush the right of the people to use a "free" sound money also should impart to us a very important lesson. If we rely on

THE GOLDEN GIFT

governments for change, as so many of us naively do, we will wait for positive change that will never come. All we will ever experience is a series of broken promises and false declarations from politicians that have mastered the art of deceit and are able to elicit religious-like fervor and blind loyalty with their masterful and carefully crafted speeches of "hope". And if by chance, a politician not hand picked by a banker slips through the cracks of the political system to become a Prime Minister or President of some nation, if this person cannot be bought with bribes, then this person will likely be targeted for elimination through a smear campaign that will force resignation, a coup to replace him, or assassination. John F. Kennedy and his brother Robert Kennedy were both murdered because their policies directly opposed those of the elite banking cartel, elite oil interests and the military-industrial complex. Is it not a coincidence that these two great men were also the last two Presidents in US history that have tried to serve the interests of the people over the interests of the bankers. Furthermore, so many among us have been so brainwashed that we still cannot see the truth despite indisputable facts that belie the true intentions of hope-spreading politicians that are nothing but wolves in sheep's clothing. Among US Presidents, Clinton, Bush, and Obama all lied to the people to hide their affiliations with the elites in power. Refer to this video, in which Obama stated, at the beginning of 2009 after explaining how huge deficits imprison all Americans and keep them downtrodden:

"We can not and will not sustain deficits like these without end. Contrary to the prevailing wisdom in Washington these past few years, we can not simply spend as we please and defer the consequences to the next budget, the next administration or the next generation. We are paying the price for these deficits

right now. In 2008 alone we paid $250 billion in interest on our debt, that is more than three times what we spent on education that year, more than seven times what we spent on VA healthcare. So if we confront this crisis without also confronting the deficits that helped cause it, we risk sinking into another crisis down the road as our interest payments rise, our obligations come due, confidence in our economy erodes and our children and grandchildren are unable to pursue their dreams because they are saddled with our debts. That's why today I am pledging to cut the deficit we inherited by half by the end of my first term in office. This will not be easy - it will require us to make difficult decisions and face challenges we have long neglected but I refuse to leave our children with a debt they can not repay. And that means taking responsibility right now in this administration, for getting our spending under control."

(Source: http://www.youtube.com/watch?v=SaQUU2ZL6D8)

Of course, if you are someone that erroneously believes that we elect Presidents and Prime Ministers and that elections are not just a ruse by the powerful men that run our countries to present to us an illusion of choice, then you may have listened to Obama's speech in 2009 and thought to yourself, *"This is a President that will fight for my rights. This is a President that understands me."* If you already understood how the political/banking machine works, then when you heard this speech, after seeing Obama appoint nearly every criminal bankster possible to his Presidential Cabinet and economic taskforce, then you would have thought, *"I bet by the end of his second term, the deficit will not be cut in half, but that it will have grown significantly."* What has been the result since Obama's promise to cut the national debt in half? When

THE GOLDEN GIFT

Obama took office, the national debt was $10.636 trillion. Cutting this in half would have reduced the debt to about $5.32 trillion. Instead, as of August, 2012, the US national debt grew to about $15.93 trillion, about 200% higher than Obama promised. What we need to understand is that it wouldn't have mattered if the US President's name was Obama, Osama, Fernandez, Lee or Smith. He would have given the same speech as Obama with the exact same result. Furthermore, the above US national debt figure is the "official" government figure and does not include trillions of more unfunded government liabilities that actually make the real national debt figure multiples higher of this fake number.

There are many among us that would like to see the implementation of a true gold standard, something that NONE among us have ever experienced in our lifetime. Those of us that truly understand who creates money, why they create it, and how the current unsound and immoral monetary system operates should understand that the most powerful Central Bankers worldwide will never instigate a TRUE gold standard ever again of their own free will (and all of you that are reading this book should understand this). Some have told me that they believe that using the word immoral to describe our current monetary system is too strong of a word. Most of these people have been employees of the banking industry. In response, I ask them to describe to me, step by step, the process of how Central Banks create money and how that money passes through the system to finally arrive in their bank account. Not one of the dozens of people that protested my use of the world immoral can do so. Not one. Thus again, we have people exercising their memory but not the grey matter inside their skulls. If they can state that a process that they can't even explain is not immoral, then I wonder what other judgments they have also made about things they do not understand. Thus, I tell every person that believes the banking system today to be moral to do one homework assignment. Research and understand how Central Banks create a bank note, and then every step after its creation to its arrival in your bank account. I tell them that once they can understand this, they will no longer have any doubt that our current monetary system is immoral. But until they can explain this to me, I tell them they have no right to protest my labeling of the system as immoral, as one of two things can only develop from this understanding. Either:

(1) This person will cease calling the banking system we use today as moral; or
(2) This person will cease being moral.

Today, the vast majority of us passively resign ourselves to participating in the fraudulent and immoral monetary system that the bankers currently impose upon us, but I am here to tell you that this does not need to be the case. Bankers are perpetually dreaming up scams devised to keep us chained to their unsound monetary system. I believe that bankers designed paper gold and paper silver ETFs (specifically the GLD and SLV) to deliberately divert money away from REAL physical gold and REAL physical silver into another bogus and fraudulent paper and digital product (just like their monetary system). Even though I have been raising concerns about the GLD and SLV being banker manufactured vehicles for the express intent of suppressing gold and silver prices for many years now, many people incredibly still believe that these two funds are legitimate investment vehicles. As of August 2012, investors had still respectively poured nearly $66B and $8.6B

THE GOLDEN GIFT

into the GLD and SLV ETFs. That's a considerable amount of private retail and institutional money that would NOT have gone into the fraudulent commercial banking system and instead should have been used to purchase REAL PHYSICAL gold and silver. If you are still invested in the GLD and/or SLV, you need to ensure that you understand the reason why US hedge fund manager David Einhorn of Greenlight Capital divested 100% of his firm's several million shares of the GLD ETF in July, 2009 and exchanged all of the cash proceeds for REAL physical gold bullion (Source: Kishan, Saijel, 2009. Greenlight Holds Bullion, Buys Reinsurance Stock. Retrieved May 10, 2012 from *the Bloomberg* website: http://www.bloomberg.com/apps/news?pid=newsarchive&sid=a16aPkJLxw0w).

For current owners of the GLD or SLV that still remain skeptical of the above, if we ever seriously hope to end our current unsound and unfair monetary system AND achieve the free market gold/silver prices we all desire, I truly believe that we will all have to divest and exchange all of our GLD and SLV ETF holdings for REAL physical gold and silver. If I'm wrong, what do you have to lose by doing so? Nothing. And if just 10% of you do so, then this small percent of divestment will probably be adequate to prove my hypothesis that the GLD and the SLV are INDEED fraudulent investment vehicles. However, there is a huge downside to NOT acting. And for those that believe in the validity of the GLD and the SLV because their custodians are the big banks of HSBC and JP Morgan, given that in 2012, HSBC and JP Morgan have both been caught engaging in numerous criminal activities from laundering money for drug cartels and terrorist countries to inside trading and deliberate mispricing scandals, this trust is highly misplaced. If I am right and those that own only paper shares of GLD and SLV do not convert them into real physical gold and real physical silver, if these ETFs are proven to be fraudulent, then those invested in them may lose 100%+ of their investment. I know that bankers claim that the GLD and SLV ETFs are 100% backed by gold and silver, but we must remember that just a few years ago, Morgan Stanley informed clients that they had purchased physical silver for them during the period of 1986-2007 and were later alleged to have purchased ZERO PHYSICAL SILVER for them, resulting in a class action lawsuit and a $4.4 million cash settlement to their clients. (Source: Bansal, Paritosh, 2007. Morgan Stanley to Settle Class Action Lawsuit. Retrieved May 10, 2012 from *the Reuters* website: http://www.reuters.com/article/2007/06/12/idUSN1228014520 070612).

Thus, just because bankers tell you something is true, this should NEVER serve as sufficient reason to believe it. Ben Bernanke, head banker and Chairman of the Federal Reserve, testified before US Congress in July, 2011 that *"[Gold] is not money"* despite 5,000 years of history and civilizations that disagree with his statement. We can start to break the bankster scam of paper gold and paper silver only if all of you reading this book take the very small action of convincing everyone you know that is invested in the GLD and SLV ETFs to exchange their investments in these funds for real physical gold and real physical silver. If you can't convince your friends that are holding GLD and SLV that these two products are likely scams, then appeal to their greed. Private independent dealers' storage fees often run considerably less than the storage fees charged by these two ETFs every year, so from a vantage point of strict profits, owning physical bullion over the ETFs makes more sense as well. And remember from

THE GOLDEN GIFT

the Morgan Stanley class action lawsuit above that storage fees do not serve as proof that allocated bullion has been purchased. Morgan Stanley charged storage fees for silver purchased for all clients named in the class action lawsuit above though they allegedly never purchased any physical silver.

When more and more of us start to own physical gold and physical silver as a means of protecting our wealth and STOP buying paper contracts bankers have invented to keep us away from buying and owning real gold and real silver, whether those paper contracts are futures, euros, or US dollars, the bankers will finally receive the message that we will not live under a system of monetary enslavement. **But not until then.** In 2011, in the futures markets, bankers sold about 100 ounces of paper gold for every ounce of REAL physical gold that exists and roughly 170 ounces of paper silver for every ounce of REAL physical silver that exists. In 2012, the banksters were trading roughly 100 million ounces of paper silver every day, or the equivalent of the total PHYSICAL supply of 1 billion ounces of silver every 10 days! However, remember that much of silver is consumed or industrial and jewelry purposes every year. Thus only about 270 to 280 million ounces of silver supply are available for monetary consumption every year. When you realize that the banksters trade 280 million ounces of paper silver every 2.8 days in the silver futures market, it is self-evident that these paper markets are fraudulent. For those that may find it incredible that banksters may actually be committing fraud on such a massive scale, I have but one refutation to present. The entire monetary system is a fraud and banksters in Europe, the US, Japan, China and all around the world have been creating trillions of their own fiat digital currencies out of thin air for the past several years. If we can understand this, and I think we all can by now, then how can we possibly refuse to believe that bankers are not committing massive fraud in the gold and silver markets? In fact, we could very legitimately argue that the act of bankers selling gold and silver that does not exist tops their rather extensive list of despicable fraudulent acts.

The reason that I urge of all you that are reading this book to take action upon your newly gained knowledge to unite with us in our fight to free ourselves from the banksters is because I truly believe that we, the people, can restore honor and integrity to the commercial banking and investment system. Furthermore, I sincerely believe that only we, and not our governments, can free ourselves from the immoral grip of banksters. Thus, it is up to us, and only us, to take the necessary actions to do so. If I didn't believe that we could collectively make a difference, I truly would not have taken the time to write this book. Furthermore, I truly hope that you participate in our efforts to make the knowledge I have presented in this book go viral, as I will be donating not only 100% of the proceeds of first year sales of this book, but also from two other books I have written, to three orphanages and children's charities that I've outlined in the book's Addendum. Thus, we can all participate in initiatives to educate the world and at the same time, help the lives of hundreds of children. I believe that I can serve as the spark to return our societies to free market capitalism and integrity from the immoral, rigged markets we have today, but I will need not only the help of everyone that reads this book, but I will also require the help of all of your friends, colleagues and family as well. I cannot stress enough the importance of not just being "willing", but also of actually "doing". We will never restore our freedoms by merely saying that we are "willing". We must also "do".

THE GOLDEN GIFT

During my life's mission of restoring sound money and freedom and of returning honesty and integrity to banking, I have met perhaps thousands of people that profess their willingness to help restore our freedoms but that never take the much more important next step of "doing." So I urge of you to take the steps I outline in this book to maximize our chances of restoring a sound monetary system to the world. Fear is one of the greatest deterrents in our decision to remain passive victims of this unjust monetary system. Some have argued that only a full-blown revolution in which people violently rout all bankers out of every dark shadow and crevice of government is the only solution that can possibly reinstate honesty into our global financial system. I do not agree. I believe that real progress and revolution can be achieved through peaceful terms and I will propose two such solutions that can possibly bring about peaceful revolution. Though the situation may look impossible to win today as we are severely outmanned by the trillions of monetary resources the banking cartel possesses to fight us, we must always remember that nothing is ever as impossible as it may first appear. I'm sure to those that fought the putrid system of Apartheid in South Africa that the achievement of equality and freedom likely appeared unwinnable and impossible at first. But eventually that battle was won by the righteous and by those that possessed only a fraction of the monetary resources as those in power. At the heart of every revolution is love, and love is force a million more times powerful than hate, greed and all the money in the world.

If we wish to achieve something, with persistence and the attitude of never ever giving up, I sincerely believe that anything is achievable. And what better goal to have than to abolish this world of a despicable system of financial slavery and to give the world and future generations a chance for peace, prosperity, and happiness that it currently will never have under our present banking system. I believe that violent revolution will be an inevitable consequence of our inaction, rather than of our action. Violent revolution may become the only viable solution to the great percent of the public if we do not apply our knowledge and convert our willingness into action right now. We have perhaps a 1-2 year window to achieve peaceful revolution that will soon be shut. Given the financial developments since the overt signs of our crisis in 2008, the path that bankers have chosen for the entire world is crystal clear. Their steadfast unwavering commitment to currency devaluation and expansion of government debt worldwide is a sign that they have deliberately chosen to demote as many of the middle class into the ranks of the poor as possible in the coming years. Thus, if you are among those that wish for peaceful revolution, as am I, the time for talking is over. The time for action is NOW and we cannot afford to wait any longer, not even for another day. A wise person of any age will understand that a proactive stance during a moderate period is far more likely to protect and preserve his or her wealth as well as his or her freedom than a reactionary stance to a severe crisis. Given that the banking cartel is hell-bent on financially destroying as many people as possible, the window for peaceful revolution is quickly closing. If you believe I am being an alarmist or exaggerating the severity of this current crisis, then please read this excerpt from Milton Mayer's book <u>They Thought They Were Free</u> in which Mayer explains how the brutal dictatorship of Nazi Germany came into being despite the presence of millions of honest, good people that chose to remain passive and do nothing:

THE GOLDEN GIFT

"What happened here was the gradual habituation of the people, little by little, to being governed by surprise; to receiving decisions deliberated in secret; to believing that the situation was so complicated that the government had to act on information which the people could not understand, or so dangerous that, even if the people could not understand it, it could not be released because of national security. And their sense of identification with Hitler, their trust in him, made it easier to widen this gap and reassured those who would otherwise have worried about it."

I have spent the last decade closely studying political and financial developments in the US and the EU and much of what has already happened and is in the process of happening right now, i.e., the decisions made behind closed doors that are sprung and forced upon people (the massive banker bailouts, the proposed European Stability Mechanism), the constant propaganda that we must leave these decisions about how to solve economic deterioration to our "leaders" because it is too complex for the general public to understand, the gradual stripping away of liberties and rights under the false context of "national security", the increasing use of the monetary system to strip away wealth from the people so that people cannot rebel, etc. – these are the exact same developments that allowed Hitler and his cronies to force the repressive policies of the Third Reich upon millions of Germans. Those that have not studied Nazi Germany may believe that the brutal dictatorship of Hitler happened overnight, but in reality, Hitler rose to power on the back of very subtle transformations in society over time, much as is the case happening in many countries today. This is why, we must choose to stand in solidarity with our brothers and sisters of all colors, races, religions and creeds, and fight the criminal banking cartel today before we head past the point of no return. Bankers are experts in artificially creating crises to consolidate their power as they did in 2008, and the optimal time to fight back is never in the midst of a severe crisis. The time to do so is before the banksters heap upon us another global economic crisis of epic proportions that will dwarf the 2008 crisis as surely they will. If we remain passive until the next severe global economic crisis occurs, peaceful revolution will likely no longer be a viable solution.

Today many people refuse to get involved in our fight for freedom, because they fear governments and they fear banksters. Today, many people are even afraid of publicly stating their opinion or opposition to the highly immoral banking cartel for fear of being placed on some government "black list" or for fear of being shunned by their neighbors, or worst of all, for fear of losing one's job. But I ask you this. Is losing one's job worse than losing one's freedom and sentencing your children and your grandchildren to a life of misery and financial slavery? We must not let fear suppress our righteousness and morality. Instead, we must allow our love for humanity to conquer our fear of banksters. It is only when we allow love to drive our behavior that it is possible to build a better life for ourselves. If we allow fear to drive our behavior, we cannot possibly hope to build a world that is worthy of our presence.

Please consider that the joy all of us will experience from living even a single year free of the chains and burdens imposed upon us by our current unsound monetary system. Because none among us have even walked a single day free of these chains, a single year will produce more joy than any of us can imagine. And if one year could produce unimaginable

THE GOLDEN GIFT

joy, what about 10 years or 20 years of life free of these monetary burdens? So are the rewards worth the risks? Ultimately I don't believe that the answer is even a choice, but rather our moral imperative to do everything within our power to help establish a new, just, moral and sound monetary system that will benefit all of humanity and fill this world with love. For if we do not, our passivity will hurt not only our own generation, but will also punish the next few generations as our passivity will likely usher in such a repressive monetary system in coming years that future generations will be without the opportunity to make any of the choices available to us right here, right now. The choice of becoming involved in creating a legitimate monetary system for the world is simply the choice between freedom and slavery. If this current situation devolves into one in which the bankers destroy the Euro or USD and then disingenuously pretend to come to our rescue by creating a "new" currency for the world, I guarantee you with 100% certainty that any "new" monetary system presented to us in the future will be one that is exponentially more oppressive than our current one.

Before I embark on the discussion of my simple solution that I believe can spark a spiritual revolution that will cleanse and purify our currently unethical global banking system, let me begin with a short parable. Today people are addicted to the idea that our current unsound monetary and banking system is a fair and equitable system. The purpose of this parable is to trigger recognition of the monetary problem the whole world faces today in simple terms with a simple story. Hopefully all people, young and old, formally educated, home schooled, and schooled on the streets, can understand this short parable. The first step to recovery is always recognition of the problem. The second step to recovery is belief that we have the power to force positive change. Everyone single one among us that has tasted a bit of success, whether as an entrepreneur, whether in our pursuit of a dream with slight odds of success in entertainment or professional sports, or whether surviving gravely negative circumstances during war or as refugees, has heard the words "it can't be done" repeatedly throughout his or her life. Yet, we all chose to ignore those words and those doubts heaped upon us to accomplish something that so many people told us could not be done. Collectively, think of how impossibly futile a task it would be for banksters to stop us from tearing down their immoral banking system and reconstructing a new, sound, moral one if 6.8 billion of us united with the resolve to positively change this world? So without further delay, let me present to you a modern monetary fable.

THE GOLDEN GIFT

CHAPTER SIX
A Modern Monetary Fable: The Realization of Monetary Truth Exposed by the Absence of Money - Lost...with a Banker

Imagine that you have just embarked on a week-long holiday aboard a cruise ship in the Caribbean. Suddenly a vicious storm descends upon the beautiful azure seas and a rogue wave swallows your boat and capsizes it. You are among a lucky group of a thousand people that manages to escape on lifeboats in the nick of time right before the cruise ship descends into a watery grave. Though the seas are stormy, everyone fortunate enough to make it to a lifeboat is able to successfully navigate the precarious waters and eventually reach a nearby remote, unmapped island. Unfortunately, because the ship sank so quickly, search crews quickly give up their search and rescue mission and tragically assume that all travelers were unable to escape the powerful undertow of the sinking cruise ship. With no communication devices, none of the thousand survivors, including you, have any realistic prospect of being discovered and rescued in the immediate future. However, some good news exists to partially offset the bad. The island upon which you have taken shelter is rich in small game and fruit and surrounded by waters teeming with fish. Starvation will not be anyone's fate.

After the initial shock of your situation wears off, with no hope of rescue anytime in the foreseeable future, you and your companions decide to begin the process of making a new life for yourselves on your remote island. A meeting is convened to establish ground rules for your new community. A banker named Hank leads the meeting and your community quickly reaches a consensus that one of the first necessities is the establishment of a system to trade for goods and services.

Hank holds up a small rectangular piece of red cotton cloth for all to see.

"I happened to be dropping off a shipment of red t-shirts when our cruise ship sunk," Hank shouts. "It's a small miracle, but I found two cartons washed upon the south beach last week that contained some of my shirts. I have cut each shirt into 50 of these rectangles. If we say each piece of red cloth is the equivalent of one island dollar, we now have 50,000 'island dollars' for use in buying goods and services on this island."

A lean Latino man with curly brown hair raises his hand to pose a question.

"Yes," Hank says.

"And what will we use these pieces of money for?"

"Everything," Hank replies. "The fruit on this island is free and so is whatever small game you can catch yourself, but some of us have already gathered seeds from the edible plants on this island and have begun planting additional crops. If you want to supplement your diet with this food, you will use this money to buy food from our farms. We have engineers and construction workers among us that have already crafted some

THE GOLDEN GIFT

tools with which they can build dirt roads to make travel more accessible around the island. We will pay them for their labor with this money."

A teenage girl interrupts. "Wait, wait, wait. Not so fast Hank. Who will determine how many pieces of island money will be needed to buy food every year? Say I want a crate of pineapples. How much will that cost?"

"One island dollar."

"Well what about the next year?" the girl questions.

"Still one island dollar."

"And what about when we run out of all 50,000 island dollars?" the Latino man asks. "That doesn't seem like a lot of money for a thousand people to use. What will we use then?"

"Don't worry," Hank implores. "We may run out of red shirts but we can make more money out of other color shirts."

"And who decides how much more money is created?" a brunette teenager with high cheekbones named Maria yells out.

"I will."

"You will?" Maria challenges Hank. "Why should you decide? And what if another one of your crates of red t-shirts washes up on the beach and someone else finds and doesn't tell anyone? Or what if someone creates their own money out of thin air by dying a white t-shirt red?"

"Let them keep it. Just chalk it up to good fortune or ingenuity and let them keep their fortune."

"They can make their own money and no one will know?" a faceless voice pipes up from inside the crowd. "How is that fair? You may say that's ingenuity but I say that's deceit!"

"Look people," Hank calmly responds. "Remember hearing about the sovereign debt crisis on the news when we were still connected to the outside world? How do you think these debt crises came to be? Governments all over the world didn't have money to pay the interest on their government issued bonds so they just created more money to pay the interest or made the people come up with their debt payments by inventing new taxes or increasing existing taxes. That's nothing different than someone stumbling upon another crate of my red shirts or someone creating their own money out of thin air by dying a white t-shirt red. Let them do it. It's not going to affect us that much."

"Wait, so you're saying that we should use the same system that nearly collapsed the world economy! How is that smart?" the anonymous voice speaks out again. "Or maybe you want to let someone create new money at will because you've hidden 5 more crates of red shirts to allow yourself to secretly make 225,000 more island dollars and keep it all to yourself!"

"Yeah," another 30-year old woman chimes in agreement. "And if that happens, how can that not affect us? Say we just let someone else create 225,000 more island dollars and keep it for himself. Well I'm not that good at math, but if we only

THE GOLDEN GIFT

started with 50,000 island dollars and we now have 275,000 island dollars floating around the island, I'm guessing that the crate of pineapples that only costs $1 this year will rise to $5 or more if suddenly we have five times as much money chasing the same amount of goods? Or what if the pineapple farmer decides to use some of the excess money that's been introduced on to our island to increase his production of pineapples? Due to his increased requirements of labor and land, the production cycle will increase in time, less pineapples will be produced, and the prices of pineapples will rise in the short-term before the farmer realizes that he produced too many pineapples given the demand. And when demand dries up for his surplus of pineapples, the prices of his pineapples will crash and maybe put him out of business, so that none of us will have pineapples anymore. That's bad for us. That's bad for the pineapple farmer. I don't see how anyone benefits from this system but you!"

"So what? So what if a crate of pineapples increases to $5?" Hank defensively retorts, his voice rising in annoyance. "Do you not pay more money every year for the same goods and services when you lived out there?" Hank motions very animatedly to the outside world that exists somewhere over the horizon. "The price of goods out there always rises every year. And even when they're not rising, the packaging is getting smaller for the same food item at the same price, so in reality, prices are rising though you may not think they are. And if the pineapple farmer goes bankrupt because of dumb decisions, I hate to tell you people, but businesses out there go belly up all the time too. That's just how things work."

"Man this is such rubbish!" Maria yells. "One minute ago you just told me that a basket of pineapples would be the same price next year as it is this year and the next minute, you're already backtracking and telling me I might have to pay five times as much for a basket of pineapples next year. So does that mean my employer is going to raise my salary by 400% next year to match my increase in the cost of goods?"

"Yeah," the 30-year old woman agrees. "And while people do make bad decisions and businesses fail, you don't have to implement a system that makes it as easy as possible for a business to fail. Why not implement a system that makes it hard for a person to make bad decisions and hard for a business to fail?"

The crowd erupts in protest and indistinguishable loud chatter.

"Calm down everyone. Listen up," Hank continues. "What I'm offering you is better than the system out there. The system out there creates money as debt. Bankers charge interest on every single new dollar that they create. And the government ends up charging you for that interest by slapping you with income taxes. I, on the other hand, will be creating money and providing it to you interest and debt-free. My system is much more honest."

"Honest? Man, whatever you're smoking, I want some of it," a 20-year old boy replies. "You are one highly delusional person. If this system of island dollars is better than the one out there, then I guess I just never got it before. You're saying if we let people create money whenever they want because they might find a new crate of red shirts, it's okay? Okay for whom? I say it's only okay for the people creating money. If I

THE GOLDEN GIFT

have 100 island dollars in my account and because you create more money, it costs me 5 island dollars to buy a crate of pineapples next year instead of one island dollar, you might as well come to my house and rob me!"

"And what if I need a loan to start a new business on the island? What interest rate will you give me?" Joe, the businessman yells.

"I'll take all market forces into consideration and decide a fair interest rate for everyone," Hank replies.

"Finally some good news," Joe the businessman smiles. "So my interest rate will be determined by laws of supply and demand, right? For example, if I want to build homes and supply is low and demand is high, then the interest rate I will be given will be very low, maybe 1%, right?"

"Maybe. Market forces will determine what it will be."

"And by market forces, you mean supply and demand, right?" Joe demands confirmation. "Tell me my interest rates will be determined by supply and demand forces."

"I'll take supply and demand into consideration, but there will be a lot of other factors that also go into the determination of interest rates," Hank replies. "But I'll make sure everyone gets a fair interest rate."

"Rubbish again," young Maria yells. "This clown is going to set interest rates at whatever rates he wants. Can't you all see that? He's using market forces to attempt to rationalize his artificial interest rates to us."

"Is that true Hank?" Joe the businessman replies, his face growing red with anger. "Yeah, what are these other factors?"

"Look, all of you are getting upset about nothing. My system essentially works in the same manner as the system out there!" Hank speaks more deliberately, taking care to emphasize each word for effect. "But like I said it's better. I can't just give you a loan at 1% interest, Joe, you know that. Maybe 8%, but 1%, come on?"

"No, I don't know, Hank," Joe replies, his voice rising by the minute. "If the free market says interest rates should be 1% because my risk of defaulting is practically non-existent, why should you charge me eight times as much?"

"Because one, I'm a business man just like you Joe. I have to make money too. And two, if I give out 1% loans, everyone will borrow money and it will cause prices of assets to rise too quickly. Out there Central Banks set the interest rates. You don't get to do this, so why should it be different on this island?"

"It should be different," Maria interrupts. "Because apparently the system out there is a form of slavery. If free markets say interest rates for construction loans should be 1%, then homebuilders would borrow money to build the homes we don't have. As houses get built and demand falls, then the free market will set interest rates higher and curb the supply of new houses that are built. Housing prices will not rise too quickly

THE GOLDEN GIFT

because interest rates will rise as demand falls and supply increases. If you get to set interest rates because you want to make money off of us, then housing prices will become distorted. But they won't be distorted if the free market is setting the price. Don't try to pass off your greed as something good for all of us. Why do you have to make money? Our money system should be one that benefits everyone on this island, not just a system for you to make money."

"I don't get it!" Hank screams, now visibly upset. "None of you ever got upset with the interest rates banks gave you out there, so why are you all so upset with my system? It's as fair as fair can be."

"No!" businessman Joe yells. "I guess none of us ever understood the system out there then. None of us understood that banks were giving us bogus, artificial interest rates. We thought out there, that we were receiving interest rates set by the free market, but I guess what we learned in school was a lie. You just said that the prices of everything will be determined by supply and demand. But then two minutes later you say that if the monetary supply on this island doubles that we may have to pay twice as much for a crate of pineapples even if real demand does not increase. Which one is it? And why should you be giving more money to the pineapple farmer to increase his production if there is not any increased demand for his goods? You're whole system is upside down. Under your system your greed to make money leads to an expansion of our money supply, not any increased real demand for goods. That type of system will make you rich but bankrupt us all."

133

"I agree," Joe's neighbor Robert proclaims. "If I want a mortgage and the price of my food just doubled because you are creating too much new money out of thin air, then my mortgage should be less than 1% per year. You can't benefit at our expense 100% of the time!"

"I'm not! My system benefits everyone. Granted, I'm taking a little bit more benefit, but why shouldn't I?" Hank sighs. "After all, I'm the one spending all the time to make the system work?"

"If that's the case," Robert raises his voice in disgust, "Then I elect myself as Head Banker of this island! And secondly, you shouldn't be spending any time at all deciding what interest rates should be. By spending time to make the system work, you mean you're rigging the system for your own benefit. You really think we are all stupid enough to be fooled by your smoke and mirrors game Hank? Let us negotiate between ourselves what interest rates should be and then you won't have to do any "work" at all. If Maria over there wants to lend her money to me at 1% to build homes, then let her lend money to me at 1%. That is, after all, what a free market is."

"Look," Hank states. "You guys are all fooling yourself. As I've already stated, how do you think interest rates are determined out there?" Hank furiously waves his arms and points to the horizon in the direction where he believes civilization to rest. "A Central Bank decides what interest rates you pay every year. Then Commercial Banks charge you a premium over that interest rate. And if you grow richer, you automatically get a better interest rate than someone else that is

THE GOLDEN GIFT

poorer just because you have more money. In my system, everyone will be charged the same interest rate. There will be no discrimination against the less fortunate. And we need someone to run this system and make these decisions. Otherwise our community will face financial chaos and perhaps collapse."

"Collapse?" Farmer Ed laughs. "Now you may think of me as a dumb hick farmer that you can fool with your big words and smart talk Hank, but I know one thing. You're already trying to seize power by selling us a crisis before we've even established our monetary system. And did you forget that we experienced a crisis out there in 2008 and we already saw how bankers reacted out there to help us? While they borrowed money from Central Banks nearly at zero percent interest rates, they hardly lowered our borrowing rates at all. Instead, they used their power to set interest rates to crush people's abilities to earn a living. Free markets? Lower interest rates for people that have more money? What kind of free markets were those? You guys were shady out there and you'll be shady on this island too. Guys like you don't grow a conscience overnight. And you want us to give you the exact same power to be our god? I think you're lower than a dog's belly and more rotten than the most rotten apple at the bottom of the barrel."

"I agree," Joe the businessman chimes in. "I say we let free market forces set interest rates. Why do you get to set our interest rates? Let us negotiate among ourselves to set interest rates for all loans for all purposes."

"I second that!" Maria shouts. "Free markets set interest rates, not Hank! Free markets set interest rates, not Hank! Free markets set interest rates, not Hank!"

"Our island needs central planning," Hank pleads. "Central Bankers don't let the free markets determine interest rates. Every month, a bunch of Central Bankers get together and decide whether to raise or lower interest rates…"

"and in the process, screw us by manipulating them, just like with LIBOR," Maria interrupts. "Let the free markets set interest rates and we have freedom. Nobody cares how it works out there. Obviously that system sucks more than the one you're suggesting. You might think Ed is stupid because he's a farmer and you might think the same of me because I'm only 19. But I know that the whole system you just described is 100% rubbish. If your system is so good, Hank, answer me one thing. There are one thousand of us on this island, right? You said you're starting our Bank with only $50,000 in island dollars. Even I can figure out without a calculator that that's only 50 island dollars a person. We'll run out of money about 10 seconds after you open our Bank. So if no one finds another crate of your red shirts to make new money, how do we get more money?"

"Like I said before, we can just use different colored cloth to create more. But really, there's no need to actually create more money once we run out."

"What do you mean?" Maria responds. "When we run out of money, then what do we use to buy stuff?"

THE GOLDEN GIFT

"I'll just keep a ledger of how much money everyone has. So if Farmer Ed," Hank points to Farmer Ed, "sells six baskets of pineapples for six dollars, I'll credit Farmer Ed's account on my ledger book with six dollars."

"Wait a second!" Farmer Ed yells. "If you just keep everyone's money as a recorded number in a book, how is that even real?"

"Ed, Ed, Ed," Hank shakes his head back and forth. "You really are a stupid hick farmer! How much 'real' money did you have in your bank account out there? All that money you think you have in your bank account does not physically exist. It's a digital entry on a computer and no different than the entry I will make in my ledger book to account for everyone's money on this island."

"No, no, no. You're wrong Hank. Out there, I ran a huge farm and it's a cash business. I deposited $2 million in cash over the past three years. I know I have $2 million in cash in my account that I can take out whenever I want if I ever make it back to the mainland."

"You really believe that?" Hank retorts in disbelief.

"I-I-I can't?" Ed stammers.

Hank answers more slowly this time.

"No…you…can't. That money is gone. The bank lends out all of your cash to try to make more money with it. The bank has lent out or invested all your money for their own proprietary accounts. What you see on your bank statement every month is a pure digital entry. If we ever make it back, you really think you could walk into your bank and withdraw, unannounced, $2 million in cash? What kind of fool are you?"

"Invested how?" Ed demands.

"I don't know for sure. It might be invested in credit default swaps, the stock market, financial derivatives, or mortgage backed securities. But the one place it is not, is at your bank. The number you see in your bank account every time you visit an ATM machine is just a ledger entry on the bank's computers just like it would be a ledger entry in my book here on this island. There is no difference. You have no problem out there, then you should have no problem on this island."

"You're telling me that if I ever visited that bank out there again and demanded all 2 million of my dollars that my bank couldn't produce it?" Ed questions.

"Not on the spot," Hank replies. "And I'll do what every bank in our country would do if you physically need the money that is in my ledger book. I'll create more and give it to you."

"But how? I thought all the red shirts are gone. How will you make new money?"

"Look," Hank says. "It doesn't have to be red shirts. So maybe I'll take some white shirts, wash them with red flowers, and make new island dollars that way. Or maybe Robert will have the red pieces of money stored in his account so I'll take

THE GOLDEN GIFT

it out of his account and give it to you. But I'll figure it out when the time comes. In the meantime don't worry about it."

"Don't worry about it?" Maria protests. "Don't worry that you're just pushing numbers around different accounts in a book without the money ever existing? If that's all you're doing, why do we need those stinking pieces of red cloth to begin with?"

Hank, his frustration growing at Maria's constant barrage of questions, removes a 100 dollar bill from his pocket and waves it over his head. "What gives this piece of paper any value? Anyone?"

"Gold!" an anonymous voice yells.

"You think US money is backed by gold?" Hank laughs. "Bankers are the only thing that gives this piece of paper value. Bankers tell you every month how much this piece of paper can buy. Not free markets. Not supply and demand. Not the stupid full faith and credit of governments. And certainly not gold. Just think of me as your friendly neighborhood banker. As long as I say this has value," Hank raises a strip of red cloth over his head and waves it, "and you believe me, then it has value. As long as I say that number I keep in your account on my ledger has value, then it has value. As long as I say that 20 pieces of red cloth are worth 20 times the value of one piece of red cloth, then it is. Look, if everyone in the world lost faith and belief in the USD and the Euro, both of them would have zero value tomorrow as well. Both of those currencies ONLY have any value because people believe the bankers that have ordered them to believe that a piece of paper with a higher number on it is worth more than a piece of paper with a lower number on it. You all are the fools, not me!"

Hank takes a lighter out of his pocket, holds the hundred-dollar bill high for everyone to see and sets fire to it.

"We don't even really need physical money." Hank throws the $100 bill in the air as the flames reach his fingers. "I don't care. We can just use a ledger if you want. That's fine by me. Have not any of you been following the news out there? Governments all over the world are moving to a cashless society. Spain has already demanded that payments in excess of 2,500€ be paid only digitally and not in cash. The entire system out there is based upon belief in us, the bankers."

"That's the problem," Maria yells. **"WE DON'T BELIEVE YOU!"**

"But if you can create an infinite amount of money out of thin air as just ledger entries on a book," an older man interrupts, "then won't all the money on our island be essentially worthless? And won't the money we already own on your ledger lose value very single year?"

"This ain't wonderland and we ain't your Alices!" a skater boy yells.

"No, no, no!" Hank firmly repudiates the protestors. "Have any of you been listening to anything I've been saying for the last hour? This," Hank digs out another 100 dollar bill from his pocket and furiously shakes it, "can buy goods and services out there. There is no difference, from an operational standard,

THE GOLDEN GIFT

between this and the numbers of island dollars each of you retain in my ledger! How many times do I have to tell you that what I'm offering you is better. I'm creating my – I mean OUR – money, debt-free. I'm not making any of you pay interest on the island money that I create. That means that our money will keep its value way better than the money out there."

The crowd's murmurings become more hostile. "But your system still sucks. You decide interest rates on the loans we receive. You decide how much money should be created and how many goods and services our money can buy every year. You basically decide if we are wealthy or poor every year! And you create production of goods and services that may not even be necessary if you slash interest rates. You may be creating debt-free money but you are creating a system that allows you to indiscriminately steal our wealth with impunity!" an elderly voice protests. "If you're system is better than the system out there as you insist it is, wow. What a criminal system you guys must have forced us to use out there."

"Let's elect a new leader," a much younger voice interjects. "We don't need another crook running our bank! Robert for Bank President!"

"Listen to me, please!" Hank protests. "Please!"

The crowd's murmurs become more intense and angry. Jimmy, a young teenager of 19, hops on top of a wooden crate so the crowd can hear him.

"You ain't our king and we ain't your slaves," he yells at Hank. "That's the craziest, most insane monetary system that I've ever heard of. No sane person would ever accept your proposal."

"You just called yourself insane!" Hank yells, his face turning red with anger. "Because you accepted a system out there worse than the one I just proposed!"

"No!" Jimmy yells back at Hank. "I was never insane! An insane group of men like you just got control over our monetary system out there and lied, cheated and stole from us for 100 years. I just never understood how evil your system was before today. But now that I understand, I only serve one God and you are not Him. You can't decide for us the quantity of goods and services our money will buy every year. You can't tell me that next year, I can work harder than I did this year, make more money, but still be poorer because my money will be able to buy less goods on this island. I might as well be your slave. And I'll tell you right now, there's no way what you're proposing is going down. Not on my watch. I'll whip your butt right now if I have to."

"Stupid kid," Hank mutters under his breath. "What kind of system do you think you've lived under for the first 19 years of your life? You --"

The crowd explodes into agreement after Jimmy finishes his speech and drowns out Hank's thoughts.

"Jimmy! Jimmy! Jimmy!"

THE GOLDEN GIFT

"You all don't know anything!" Hank angrily screams, trying desperately to be heard over the ruckus of the crowd. "You think you're so smart. You need me to tell you how our monetary system should work. All of you want to be heroes, but without me, you'll have nothing but failure and chaos and you'll all be fighting each other before this year is even over. You won't even last a year."

"No," Jimmy replies. "Without you, you arrogant sociopath, the only thing we will be missing is massive fraud and deceit. Without you we'll have freedom. Without you, we'll have peace for years. Welcome to reality, Hank. I move to build the First Island Penitentiary, just for our first resident, Hank. Who's with me?"

The crowd erupts in cheers and chases Hank from the meeting.

THE END

After reading the above parable, I hope you understand that the root of nearly all economic problems today, whether it is unemployment or the strong possibility of sovereign debt default, is an unsound monetary system. Though a crook by any definition, former US President Nixon was halfway on the mark when he stated, *"the strength of a nation's currency is based on the strength of that nation's economy."* Given the precarious nature of the Yen, the Pound Sterling, the Euro and the US dollar, the US, the UK, Japan and the entire European Union are in reality among the weakest economies in the world now. However, a much more accurate statement than Nixon's would be that the strength and soundness of a nation's currency dictates, rather than is based on, the strength of a nation's economy. As I stated earlier, those that actually realize how the monetary system truly operates know that the bankers wish to keep this false system of legalized deceit and bamboozlement in operation en perpetuity. However, it is a massive mistake to assume that we are powerless to change this system.

A few banking families, as much of the world's wealth as they own, do not have the power to stop nearly 7 billion people from implementing a new monetary system. They only maintain this power because nearly 7 billion people DO NOT UNDERSTAND how the current monetary system works and we willingly participate in this system. All it takes to destroy the conditions of financial enslavement that they impose upon us is our refusal to participate and help their system. Though these banking families wish for you to believe the fairytales they teach in business school such as the existence of free markets, fair equity and fair real estate markets, transparent capitalism, and the idea that everyone has an equal shot at achieving their dreams of riches and great wealth if they would only pull themselves up by their bootstraps, such notions are patently absurd. Bankers, through our current fractional reserve banking system, have rigged every single capital market in existence to make it absurdly easy for themselves to build, maintain and sustain their wealth while making it absurdly difficult for anyone else to do the same. This is why you have seen so many stories of millionaires and billionaires that go bankrupt and then have to rebuild their fortunes again. The first time, or first several times they went bankrupt, they did not understand the monetary system. After they finally understand it, this is when they are able to sustain and keep their wealth. By remaining passive and allowing banker-

THE GOLDEN GIFT

controlled governments to mandate the course of societal change, we unfortunately have transformed the absurd into a sad reality (Read The Atlantic magazine article, "*The Quiet Coup*", by Simon Johnson to understand how bankers have gained control of governments. You can find the link in the Reference page at the end of this book). The time to change our sad reality of enslavement into a more positive one of freedom is well overdue.

JS KIM

CHAPTER SEVEN
The Solution - Project Sound Money

With massive daily stock market fraud, rigged real estate markets, and rigged commodity markets pervasive throughout the world, the majority of us that have followed capital markets long enough to understand beyond a shadow of a doubt that free markets do not exist have been endlessly searching for a way to stop this monetary form of slavery that Central Bankers have imposed upon us. Governments will never free us. Bankers will never free us. But we can free ourselves. We can initiate a project that would free all project participants from the shackles of an unsound monetary system and the corrupt power of bankers. The rich, middle class, and poor will ALL flourish much more significantly under a fair, transparent, equitable sound money system. The only people that will be opposed to this project and idea are the few thousand men and women that own the Central Banks of this world and the banking executives at commercial banks, because for the first time in their lives, they will have to actually work to earn wealth instead of merely stealing it from everyone else (in both a figurative and a literal sense).

And perhaps such a project can show the rest of the world that they can be free as well. A project undertaken by a community of a few thousand people would illustrate to the world that we can indeed free ourselves from the power of bankers to steal our wealth with impunity, as they do now.

THE GOLDEN GIFT

And if we can illustrate to the world that our current banking system is just a legalized criminal system of continual theft, then we can ensure that any banker that ever tries to instill such a system again at any point in the future will spend the rest of his or her life in jail. The current monetary system as it exists in its current form is a crime upon humanity far greater than the Holocaust, for this system imposes deliberate and unnecessary suffering and hardship upon nearly 7 billion people. This statement is not meant to belittle the grave atrocities of the Holocaust that ushered in the deaths of between 11 million to 17 million Jews, Russians, Polish, and other ethnic minorities, but rather to emphasize the immorality of a system that negatively impacts billions and has indirectly lead to deaths *many multiples the amount* of those the Holocaust created. Any person of any race, culture, or religion that has ancestors that were exploited should be ashamed of himself if he works for the banking industry knowing that he is part of a system that exploits all of humanity on an exponentially more reprehensible scale than any other historical atrocity. And any board of any pro-humanitarian organization should kick off any banker that is a member of their board as having one on their board severely soils the legitimacy of their organization.

Our current banking system is a criminal entity that needs to be demolished from the top down as it is an entity that is rotten from the top all the way to its core. While lower level employees may be ignorant of the immorality of their industry, there is no doubt in my mind that the alpha-banksters know exactly of the grave, immoral crimes they are committing against humanity. Thus, in the process of tearing down this immoral banking system step by step, we should be cautious also to honor the process of justice. Whether these alpha-banksters are still employed as bankers or perhaps employed now as academics or government officials, we should have the right to prosecute every single last one of these banking criminals for their current and past atrocities upon humanity during the implementation of a return to sound money, in order to provide a public deterrent to the potential future corruption of a new sound monetary system. While many of you that have a much greater understanding than I of city planning and the legal complexities of building a new society may justifiably criticize some of the flaws in my proposed solution, I present the solution of Project Sound Money only as an attempt to open up dialogue that can pave the way for the return of a gold and/or silver-backed sound monetary system to societies all over the world. In pondering the question of how to return the world to a sound monetary system, I have actually thought of two potential solutions that can override the rampant immorality and power of those in charge of our current global monetary system. The first one I present here, and the second one, I present in my companion book, <u>The Bankers' Secret Plot to Bankrupt the World & How We Can Stop Them!</u> The solution that I present here, while I believe it to be solid from a theoretical framework, is definitely the more difficult of the two from an applicability standpoint, given its logistical complexities and difficulties.

Still, I present this plan, dubbed Project Sound Money, in the hopes that those of you that read about this plan will start a dialogue on the Internet regarding the merits and flaws of this project for all to read. My hope, in publishing this plan, is to merely provide a spark that will foster a viral discussion worldwide about the immoralities of our present monetary system and to have these discussions eventually yield a working, sustainable solution to reinstate a sound monetary system, whether it incorporates facets of the two solutions I present in this book and my companion book, or whether it evolves from a totally separate and independent concept. However, I do believe that the second solution I present in <u>The Bankers' Secret Plot to Bankrupt the World & How We Can Stop Them!</u> is one that can work with relatively little effort and relatively little barrier to its implementation. In any event, the important factor in our search for a solution to implement a sound monetary system is not whose idea it is, but merely that we find the solution that is the easiest to apply and that has the best chance of success. We need to instigate discussion to awaken those that have been asleep to the realities of our present ongoing monetary crisis so that we can avoid being blindsided by the imminent onslaught of wealth destruction that bankers will unleash upon billions in the near future. This onslaught has already affected hundreds of millions of people negatively but it is not too late for us to stop the insanity of these banksters from implementing their New World Disorder (NWD) before it negatively impacts billions of us. It would serve humanity's interests and behoove us all if we can put a plan and solution in motion that not only will raise awareness of the immorality of our current banking system but also derail and permanently disable it.

Often, when humanitarians are asked of their greatest wish, their answers include the end of war, the end of poverty, and the end of suffering for millions of refuges. However, if we were to end poverty without implementing a sound monetary system, a feat that I do not believe is possible, we undoubtedly would still have a massive problem of war-induced refugees. Poverty can be defeated, but only if a sound monetary system is in place. If we were to establish peace without establishing a sound monetary system, we undoubtedly would still witness huge imbalances in wealth and great suffering in most countries and any peace that was achieved in the future would be fleeting and unsustainable. Thus, I present Project Sound Money to you, not as a perfect framework for exposing the wealth-robbing nature of our current unsound monetary system, but merely as a framework for discussing solutions to rid our planet of our current parasitic monetary and banking system.

Anyone that desires to solve the world's greatest problems that does not call for the establishment of a sound monetary system as the most critical element of their plan fails to understand just how critical is the establishment of a sound monetary system towards the achievement of their goals. Reinstate sound money and we will immediately begin to see poverty alleviated, war stunted, a decline in the incidents of terrorism, violent crime rates diminish, and refugee numbers dwindle across the globe. **Reinstate sound money, and I guarantee you that progress in all these areas will occur at a faster rate than at any other time in history.** Sound money is the key to enabling all solutions to poverty, war, and the end of mass suffering. Sound money would usher in a better quality of life for all people unparalleled by even the Industrial Revolution. And for those that are solely driven by self-interest, a sound monetary system will lead to the greatest period of global economic growth in modern history. Consequently, there is something about the results of a sound monetary system that benefits everyone whether that person's interest is selfish or humanitarian.

In 2009, according to Business Week magazine, 4,715,000 millionaire households existed in the US; in Japan, 1,230,000; in Germany, 485,000; in China, 677,000; and in the UK, 430,000. Thus, in four countries alone, of the 193 countries in

THE GOLDEN GIFT

the world, there were 7,537,000 millionaire households in 2009. If only 0.066339%, or just 5,000 of these households would engage in a project I have dubbed Project Sound Money, we could forever alter the way the global monetary system operates and squash most of the financial fraud that has been imposed upon us by Central Bankers through the fractional reserve banking system. If a mere 5,000 millionaire households pooled their money and each contributed US $1,000,000 to a pooled account for Project Sound Money, this would result in a capital account of $5,000,000,000. One of the main ideas of Project Sound Money is the formation of a self-sustaining community. Obviously the larger the monetary reserve this project possesses to cope with unforeseeable expenses that may arise in the pursuit of a self-sustaining community, the better will be the odds of success. But let me continue.

In developing countries in Asia and Africa, as of a few years ago, it was possible to lease land for 30-year durations at roughly USD $1-3 per hectare/year for agriculture and livestock purposes, and for about USD $60 a hectare/year for industrial purposes. Therefore, costs to rent land for living purposes for a self-sustaining community would be nominal for a community of millionaires. The recent trend of sovereign nations like Kuwait, Qatar, China, etc. to buy up hundreds of millions of dollars of arable land for dirt-cheap prices in third world countries in Asia and Africa without the provision of benefits to the locals has often justifiably created feelings of exploitation and resentment among the locals towards outsiders. Thus, it would be imperative for the members of Project Sound Money to ensure that their community provided benefits to the locals. The political logistics of forming a self-sustaining community in this manner, of course, is much easier in theory than in practice. Still, such a project IS feasible. For cleaner logistics with less hassle from governments (who in turn are controlled by banking interests), let's assume that the members of Project Sound Money decided to purchase a large private island instead of leasing land from a government to provide the foundation of this project.

In addition, let's assume the following conditions also apply to Project Sound Money:

(1) If it is not possible to include farmers, civil engineers, architects, computer engineers, teachers, doctors, construction workers and all other professions and skill sets necessary for a self-sustaining community from a subset of willing multimillionaire participants, then additional households will be recruited to join the community with a proportional capital donation to the project.
(2) The proposed location of this self-sustaining community should already possess basic infrastructure (roads, sewage, electricity, communication, etc.)
(3) No bankers, who are currently employed by and who support the modern banking system today, or that support fractional reserve banking, shall be allowed to participate in this community.
(4) Every good and service that can be produced internally using the skill set of all project members will be produced internally. Only raw materials such as iron ore, copper, rare earth metals, etc. would be imported into this community as necessary. Alternative, green energies, including wind, hydro, and solar energies, will be used and developed whenever possible to

THE GOLDEN GIFT

minimize dependence on the outside world for energy sustainability. In instances when the textile, agricultural, electronics industry etc. can be developed internally, members of Project Sound Money will drive production and growth.

(5) Project Sound Money members will establish a large industrial sector so that all technology required by its members (televisions, computers, automobiles) can be sourced directly from its own factories.

(6) Project Sound Money will institute a bi-metal gold & silver backed standard as its monetary system using the remaining money in the $5,000,000,000 pooled capital account of its citizens (after the leasing/purchase of land required for the project) to back its money. Of this capital account, 20% will be allocated for the leasing/purchase of land and an Emergency Reserve Fund to cope with unforeseeable project expenses. Of course, if the tract of land for PSM was quite large, then the money to purchase this land would likely have to come from outside the original $5 billion reserve for this project, but if enough multi-millionaires participated in this project, then this scenario would still be possible. The remaining $4 billion of reserves will be used to purchase Good for Delivery gold and silver bars at the prevailing market price to back the creation of a new currency, The Golden. The exact percentages of this dual gold/silver standard would be determined by the prevailing prices and supply of gold/silver. Of the nearly $4 billion Goldens, each citizen of Project Sound Money will initially receive $250,000 Goldens for living expenses. The remaining Goldens will be contributed as capital to back the New

Sound Money Bank. All Goldens will be created under the authority of the Island Treasury and all Goldens will be created interest-free and with no debt component. Furthermore the Bank of Goldens will emulate the 1609 Bank of Amsterdam as its operational guide.

(7) All members of Project Sound Money will bring and service no outside debt once a member of this new community (this is merely to ensure to the outside world that any failure of any member to live comfortably within this community will not result from debt burdens that were incurred in the outside world under the immoral fractional reserve banking system). Furthermore debt-to-income ratio requirements for any loans incurred inside Project Sound Money will be much more strict than any current banking regulations in the outside world and no interest payments will be associated with the terms of any loan offered by the Bank of Goldens. All interest rates on any interest-rate bearing loan will be determined not by the Bank of Goldens, but in a free market setting, as negotiated between interested parties.

(8) There will be zero income tax assessed in this community as no income tax will be necessary to pay off banksters for interest accrued on national debt as Goldens will be created as an asset, not as a debt. 100% of any other taxes assessed within this community will provide infrastructure and education and other community services. This should minimize the necessity of Project Sound Money participants to incur large debts to grow their businesses, as more capital

THE GOLDEN GIFT

will be readily available to reinvest into organic business growth and production.

(9) Any creation of new Goldens other than the original capital established must be backed by the additional purchase of gold/silver in the percentages originally established. Any deliberate attempt to debase the valuation of Goldens through fraud, deceit, or destruction of the gold/silver backing system will automatically result in a life prison sentence with no chance of parole. In addition, Project Sound Money participants will hire private security, whose lone duty will be to protect the project from the interference of foreign governments and criminal global banking interests to ensure that all project participants shall be free to live under the new monetary system they implement. The Bank of Goldens may raise money to offset the costs of private security services through bank transaction fees. Internal governance laws shall be mutually developed with the approval of all project participants.

In support of this new monetary system, the following conditions will also apply.

Each Golden will be fully redeemable at all times in 99.999% fine gold and 99.999% fine silver. No Golden will ever be printed as debt with a third-party counterparty risk. No central bank will ever be allowed to exist or will ever be considered for establishment and all interest rates will be set by free market forces and not by any banker or any central bank. No bank in the community will be allowed to trade in derivative products, establish a proprietary trading desk or engage in any business practice besides storing money and charging fees for transactions. The Bank of Golden will only be allowed to invest money accrued above and beyond the 100% reserve ratio requirement and thus will bear 100% of the brunt of any losses associated with unsound investments. The New Sound Money Bank will not issue any credit cards for use in Project Sound Money.

The Bank of Goldens will be required to abide by a 100% reserve ratio requirement. The 100% reserve ratio requirement may not be debased or circumvented by the passage of any new legislation for any reason. The banking system of this new project will be set up to serve the interests of the people only, with minimum to no benefit for the bankers. Salaries of bankers will be capped at a rate no greater than 20% above the median salary of the community.

Given these guidelines, I believe that the following realizations would become self-evident within a few short years after the commencement of Project Sound Money. Because free markets will drive asset valuations within the Project Sound Money community, no capital market based within the project will suffer massive and artificially distorted asset prices. In the absence of severe price distortions that are commonplace in almost every capital market outside of the Project Sound Money (PSM) island, steady, sustainable and fundamentally-sound economic growth will occur within the PSM community even if financial instability and meltdowns continue to plague the outside world. Furthermore, even if

THE GOLDEN GIFT

massive bank runs afflict major global banks, any depositor of the Bank of Goldens will be 100% guaranteed to be able to withdraw 100% of all his or her deposits at anytime.

For this very reason, the economics that drive the growth of the Project Sound Money community would literally be unlike any other place on earth. Absent of economic growth, no new money would be created. Only free market forces and real organic economic growth would provide the stimulus for the creation of new money in the Project Sound Money community. No corrupt bankers would exist on PSM to create artificially-low interest rates that would give rise to severe price distortions that would eventually collapse under the weight of its own fraud. Within the Project Sound Money community, due to free market regulation of monetary supply growth rates and the abolishment of fractional reserve banking practices, the purchasing power of the Goldens would be preserved over long periods of time, and price stability could be expected even over a century's time. Given these conditions, Goldens would easily become the strongest currency in the world within a relatively short period of time.

After the establishment of the Project Sound Money (PSM) community, it is a safe bet to state that no banker-controlled government outside of this small community would ever accept Goldens as a redeemable form of currency. A small black market for goods and services that trade in Goldens may form in response to Project Sound Money. However, since the project community would be formed as a self-sustaining community, there would never be a need for any project member to ever spend Goldens outside of the PSM community. In the instances when PSM members need or desire to travel outside of the self-sustaining project, they would be able to redeem their Goldens at the Bank of Goldens for physical gold and silver, which in turn, they could convert into dollars, Euros, pounds, Special Drawing Rights (SDRs), etc. or whatever was the fraudulent reserve currency used by the outside world. However, since any PSM community member would only be converting Goldens into the fraudulent currency of the outside world for the sole purposes of immediately spending it, he or she would not be harmed by the constantly devaluing purchasing power of all other fraudulent global banking currencies. Thus, PSM community members that had an affinity for Apple products would still be able to purchase a future iPad 10.0 and the latest Apple gadgets. Furthermore, a total collapse of any fiat currency would have no detrimental bearing on the wealth of PSM community members as the value of Goldens would only rise relative to all other global banking currencies in response to such an event. Though the price of imported raw materials into the island community would undoubtedly rise in terms of outside fiat currencies, because the Golden's strength and purchasing power would also rise in terms of all outside fiat currencies, the REAL cost of imported materials to the project would still remain constant or even likely decrease in response to such a global catastrophic event.

Inflation rates within Project Sound Money would either be zero or remain near zero every year, thereby ensuring that an increase in salary would actually translate into a higher standard of living. In the outside world this is almost never the case. Corporation-granted employee salary increases, except for a rare, exceptional case, are never equal to, or larger than, the currency devaluation rates that Central Bankers inflict upon all fiat currencies every year. In fact, in most instances, even a 6% salary raise is equivalent to *a negative real rate of return* and is responsible for *a decrease in one's standard of*

THE GOLDEN GIFT

living due to the current massive global currency devaluation race to the bottom. For example, in the United States, in the eight years between 2000 and 2008, the US dollar's purchasing power fell by roughly 50% against a basket of international currencies most heavily weighted in the Euro and Yen. Therefore, if one earned USD $100,000 in salary in 2000, a doubling of one's salary to USD $200,000 by 2008 would have incredibly not improved one's standard of living, as the purchasing power of 200,000 2008-year US dollars was equivalent to the purchasing power of 100,000 2000-year US dollars. However, most people today still do not understand this simple fact and they believe that *a nominal increase* in dollars, Euros, Pounds and Yen is equivalent to *a real increase* in their wealth. It is not. This is the great lie that bankers built into our current monetary system that they depend upon you to believe in order for them to maintain this system.

The wealth increase of Project Sound Money citizens *not just in nominal terms but also in real terms* over time would shed massive light on the scam of our current banking system and eventually, such a situation would lead the rest of the world to question why the standard of living was increasing for every subsequent generation of the PSM community as their standard of living was simultaneously decreasing. Thus, if PSM community members earned G$100,000 in 2015 (G for Goldens) and then earned G$150,000 by 2018, their standard of living would have increased tremendously as opposed to citizens outside of the PSM community that may have received similar increases in fiat currency based salaries.

So how would significant improvements in the standard of living for 5-6,000 households help the rest of the world? Here's the answer. Every year, Project Sound Money, depending upon the acreage of the land originally purchased for the project, would open up a wait list for a limited number of families to join the project, this time absent of any net wealth criteria. After a little bit of press and publicity, due to the enormous benefits that Project Sound Money would offer all of its participants, thousands of families undoubtedly would apply for citizenship on the isle of Project Sound Money. The fact that Project Sound Money would possess the highest standard of living of any place on earth, bar none, would undoubtedly generate an enormous amount of publicity that would be very difficult to suppress, even among banker-owned channels of mass media distribution. After some time, one of these stories would almost be guaranteed to go viral. And if every single person in this world were to simultaneously realize that he or she was being duped by the current parasitic global monetary system that Central Bankers have imposed upon us, the critical mass necessary to move people from a state of inertia to action would finally develop. In theory, this is how a small project like Project Sound Money could successfully spark a monumentally positive change that would ultimately benefit the entire world's population.

Now, let's breakdown the flaws of Project Sound Money. I realize that the easiest criticism of my above project is the belief that one will find it very difficult, if not impossible, to find a group of multi-millionaires willing to fund such a project since many very wealthy people benefit from the corrupt global financial and banking system and wish to maintain the status quo versus expose our current monetary system for its immorality. For example, the ability to leverage our current immoral monetary system is the very reason why people like Americans Warren Buffet and Charlie Munger constantly criticize public ownership of gold as dumb and counter-productive when privately, their reasons for doing so

THE GOLDEN GIFT

are likely very different than the ones they publicly voice. Since people like Buffet and Munger built their fortunes leveraging our current immoral system to build their vast fortunes, they have every reason to fight a return to an honest sound monetary system that would actually level the playing field for everyone to pursue the same amount of wealth that Buffet and Munger have been able to accumulate. As one example of building wealth from the immorality of the system versus wealth built from hard labor or any iota of intelligence, Warren Buffet secured a special deal available to no other person in the world when he bought $5 billion of a preferred class of Goldman Sachs shares that guaranteed him a no-risk $1.3 million payout every single day (Source: Alden, William, Goldman Sachs Reportedly Paying Warren Buffet $1.3 Million Per Day, May Repay Investment, retrieved May 10, 2012 from *the Huffington Post* website: http://www.huffingtonpost.com/2010/10/21/warren-buffett-goldman-sachs_n_771072.html).

Throughout his career, Buffet has leveraged the fraud built into the system to build wealth, so it is understandable that a man like Buffet would never participate in a noble experiment to benefit all of humanity like Project Sound Money. Thus, the criticism of finding enough millionaires and/or billionaires to willingly participate in and fund Project Sound Money does have a lot of merit. I've also thought about how realistic (or unrealistic) something like Project Sound Money may be, given that it requires the cooperation of a lot of moving parts to have any chance of success. Because Project Sound Money may be a project that would be very difficult to implement in real life and because it undoubtedly would receive enormous opposition from governments that would attempt to shut it down before it even got started, I have also formulated a second solution that can also re-instate Sound Money that relies far less on the centralized execution of a plan by an elite group of people whose best interests may not be served by such a plan.

In fact, my second solution can easily and seamlessly incorporate the equal participation of all socio-economic classes, is absent of the logistical barriers of Project Sound Money and can also be executed from a decentralized platform. The only barriers to achieving success with my second solution are not logistic in nature, but purely psychological and educational. Though the barriers to my second plan are only psychological and educational, due to more than a century of bankster propaganda and brainwashing, these barriers can be just as formidable as the logistical barriers of Project Sound Money. However, I want to stress that formidable hardly translates into impossible. Formidable only means that we will have to put forth sincere, dedicated and persistent efforts to be successful. As I've stated earlier, I will present my second solution in my companion book, <u>The Bankers' Secret Plan to Bankrupt the World & How We Can Stop Them!</u> – a book I plan to release just a couple of months after the release of this one.

Finally, I want to illustrate that despite the logistic complexities of instituting such an ambitious project such as Project Sound Money, as I discussed earlier in this book, the Malaysian state of Kelantan has already successfully instituted some aspects of my Project Sound Money at a micro level. On August 12, 2010, the Malaysian state of Kelantan started issuing Gold Dinars and Silver Dirhams according to Shariah law as an alternative to fraudulent paper Malaysian ringgit fiat currency. Almost immediately, the first batch of gold dinar and silver dirham coins, worth about 2.36 million ringgit, sold out.

THE GOLDEN GIFT

This fact alone illustrates the tremendous support that would exist for a plan like Project Sound Money as long as people understood how such a plan would benefit them.

According to Umar Ibrahim Vadillo, the chief executive of the Kelantan Golden Trade, *"In Kelantan, businesses including garage owners and taxi drivers are using the gold and silver coins."* This fact destroys the banker created myth that only rich people prefer the use of gold and silver as money and that middle-class or poor people would not adopt gold and silver as money. Furthermore, Kelantan has allowed civil servants to request up to 25% of their salary to be paid in Gold Dinars and Silver Dirhams instead of fiat ringgits. Mr. Umar said three more Malaysian states controlled by the opposition, Selangor, Kedah and Penan, had indicated interest in minting similar coins and returning their states to a system of sound money as well. *"By the end of the year, we anticipate sales of the dinars and dirhams to hit 60 to 70 million ringgit,"* he said. The dinar coin is 4.25 grams of 22 carat (91.67% pure) gold, equivalent to about 582 ringgit when first issued in August of 2010, while the dirham is three grams of 99.999% pure silver, equivalent to about 13 ringgit when first issued. Both Islamic gold and silver coins are minted according to Islamic law standards. Though I cannot read Malay, here is the website of the Kelantan Gold Trade Sdn Bhd mint where one can find sales statistics for the Gold Dinar and Silver Dirham (http://www.dinarkel.com/). Initially, though the Malaysian government stated that the Kelantan Gold Dinars and Silver Dirhams were not legal tender within the country of Malaysia, this has not stopped the citizens of Kelantan from using both precious metals coins as money.

In response, thus far, there has been no attempt from the Malaysian government to stop the use of the gold and silver coins in Kelantan, probably due to fear of the resultant outrage among Kelantan citizens that have already greatly benefited from their use during the first year of implementation. Furthermore, the sound money experiment in Kelantan has thus far progressed as we would envision our proposed Project Sound Money would progress, with citizens of all socio-economic levels, not just the wealthy, opting to use gold and silver over fiat Ringgit due to their discovery that gold and silver money holds their value infinitely better than the bogus Ringgit fiat currency. Indeed, Kelantan citizens have re-discovered that gold and silver money contributes to a better standard of living versus the fiat Ringgit. Though this development has been ignored by the mass media in general, and only affects a small population of people within one country, this story should have been huge news. Why? Because for the first time in our lifetime, a government somewhere in the world actually gave its citizens a choice to use inflation-free money in the form of gold and silver! (Source: 2010. Malaysians welcome gold dinars and silver dirhams, Retrieved May 10, 2012, from *The National* website: http://www.thenational.ae/news/world/asia-pacific/malaysians-welcome-gold-dinars-and-silver-dirhams)

If the rest of us had the choice to preserve the purchasing power of our money by using gold and silver currencies in every day life versus using the fiat currencies we are forced to use by immoral, sociopathic bankers, I am positive that gold and silver coins would appreciate at even a much greater rate than their current rate of appreciation against the USD, Euro, Yen, Pound, and every other paper currency in the word. Sadly, because world governments deliberately make the use of gold and silver as money as inconvenient and difficult as humanly possible, convenience, along with education, is the

THE GOLDEN GIFT

number one factor that has prevented the widespread use of gold and silver coins as money.

ADDENDUM
Help the Ideas Behind "The Golden Gift" Go VIRAL & Help Deserving Children in the Process

Since we have reached the end of this book, I first want to thank each and every one of you for opening your mind enough to read this entire book. Secondly, since I have pledged every penny of profits during the first year of sales of this book to the below three organizations that benefit children, I want to give a heartfelt thanks of appreciation to each and every one of you for your contributions to these three wonderful organizations that make the lives of precious children better:

(1) Two Sisters – In 1999, Patrick Thibedi (Chamusso) founded Two Sisters as an established care centre for children orphaned through the AIDS pandemic. Two Sisters' aim is to continue to develop and expand the drop-inn centre established in 1999, making it a flagship in the Mganduzweni Trust Area in South Africa and to set standards for others to follow. Two Sisters delivers day-to-day care for orphans, whose parent(s) have died of HIV/AIDS or related illnesses, and the provision of foster homes when necessary. *Catch a Fire*, a biographical Hollywood movie starring Derek Luke and Tim Robbins, depicts the early years of Patrick's life and his struggle against the system of Apartheid in South Africa. More information about Two Sisters can be found at:
http://www.twosisters.org.za

(2) The Mulligan Project - The Mulligan Project is a non-profit organization dedicated to improving the lives of children with disabilities in Dien Ban, Vietnam. It is widely believed

THE GOLDEN GIFT

that the staggering numbers of children born with disabilities in Dien Ban are due in part to the heavy spraying of defoliants such as Agent Orange that Dien Ban endured during the war with the United States. Approximately 20 million gallons of herbicides were sprayed on Vietnam between 1962-1971. The Mulligan Project not only provides special education, physical therapy and healthcare services to an underserved and overlooked generation of children growing up without the education they deserve, but more importantly, helps these children live a life with dignity again. More information about The Mulligan Project can be found at: http://themulliganproject.org

(3) Future Light Kids – In 2007, Jennifer Lo founded Future Light Children's Home in Mae Sot, Thailand. A full time staff of at Future Light Kids provides desperately needed housing, education and security to dozens of refugee children. Currently, Jennifer is reorganizing Future Light Kids with a broader mission of extending its goal to alleviating poverty and providing education to children all over the world. More information about Future Light Kids can be found at http://www.futurelightkids.org and more information regarding the changing structural organization of Future Light Kids will be posted on our Books for Charity page at www.smartknowledgeu.com as it becomes available.

For those that wish to help us raise money for these three wonderful children's organizations or just to keep track of how much money we have raised for these three organizations, please visit us at http://www.smartknowledgeu.com where you will find a link to a donations and information page.

In conclusion, I believe that understanding the knowledge contained in this book is not enough to bring about the significant change in our monetary system that we all want. We must believe that we have the power to bring about the change we want and we must transform our knowledge into action. I 100% believe that it is a realistic and achievable goal to awaken all 6.8 billion people in this world to the criminality of our current monetary and banking system and to unite everyone on a journey out of our current economic darkness into a new monetary renaissance of a sound, just monetary system. I believe that in order to start our journey, that only 8% of us have to muster up the courage to act and that 8% will be a high enough baseline to trigger the other 91% to join us in our battle to free ourselves from the immoral shackles of the less than 1% that lord over our current monetary and banking system. There is a global consciousness that has been rising and awakening all across the Americas, Europe and Asia and it just requires a little push to turn this awakening into an unstoppable force for good.

If I didn't believe this with all my heart, I would not have spent the last two years of my life working on this book (and The Bankers' Secret Plot to Bankrupt the World & How We Can Stop Them!) until 2AM and 3AM in the morning nearly every day and often on weekends as well. Both these books have been a labor of love, so I sincerely hope, with all my heart, that you will not just "know" about the immorality of the global banking system now, but that you will "apply" your knowledge to help free the world of the immoral grip of the banking cartel. I honestly believe that no person in the world would stand for our current monetary system if only he or she understood how an honest sound monetary system could provide a previously unimaginable standard of living for all

THE GOLDEN GIFT

global citizens and how our current monetary system is the root of almost all suffering on the planet today.

There can be no greater gift to the world, in my opinion, than the implementation of a Sound Monetary system worldwide. Though I've already made this point, I want to emphasize again that I believe that the implementation of a Sound Monetary system would quickly stimulate the most immediate and significant progress in solving poverty, refugee crises, hunger, war and terrorism that the world has ever seen in addition to raising the standard of living for all of humanity at the greatest pace in modern history since the Industrial Revolution.

If you understand the arguments I have presented in this book or take the time to research them more on your own, then I believe that you will understand that a gold and silver standard can help solve many of the world's greatest problems better than any other strategic move. During the 19th century and the early part of this century, the immorality of our current banking system was common knowledge among not only the people but also among politicians. Since then, as Pol Pot and Chairman Mao once attempted to wipe out the history of their respective nations during their tyrannical reigns, bankers have worked tremendously hard to wipe out the history of their tyranny from our history books as well. We need to re-learn this "lost" knowledge. In today's history books used in classrooms throughout the world, you will find no mention of how bankers deliberately caused the Great Depression by contracting the money supply in the 1920s with the exception of books used by a handful of Austrian economics schools. If you study the roots of the Great Depression and the global economic crisis of 2008, you will find that not only are the roots exactly the same, but you will find that the results of bankers consolidating their power in the aftermath of both crises are exactly the same as well.

Though not all among us may be courageous, there is courage among numbers. Therefore, the most courageous of us must step forward now and provide an example to the less courageous. This is a numbers game. The more people understand the fact that there will NEVER be a solution to war, poverty, refugees, crime and terrorism without first implementing a SOUND MONETARY SYSTEM, the more people will eventually step forward and join our movement to establish a sound monetary system. Every politician and banker-proposed financial "reform" that refuses to honor us with a sound monetary system is a ruse and should properly be viewed with scorn and derision as these "reforms" are only smoke screens designed to appease the masses while providing no benefits to humanity whatsoever.

Anthropologists have determined that a rough threshold for knowledge to spread throughout an entire community is a mere EIGHT PERCENT. That is why I mention this percentage numerous times as the trigger number. Our goal of spreading knowledge and truth to only 8% of our communities should be sufficient to awaken 100% of our communities. If I had to venture a guess today, I would guess that only 2% or so of people have been awakened thus far. So we are, as an estimate, only 6% away from our desired trigger point. With that in mind, I encourage all you to tell your friends to buy this book from our SmartKnowledgeU website, as I am committed to donating all first year sales profits of this book and <u>The Bankers' Secret Plot to Bankrupt Humanity & How We Can Stop Them!</u> to the three wonderful charities listed in this addendum. However, if your friends cannot afford to buy this book, then I certainly encourage you to pass this book onto

THE GOLDEN GIFT

them after you finish reading it, as the truth of our monetary and banking system is much too important not to share with as many people as possible. Together, we can change how our modern monetary system operates and give a "golden gift" to all future generations.

I have no doubt that a true gold standard maintained 100% of the time would promote steady economic growth and an increase of wealth among all socio-economic classes of all countries. Sound money is an absolutely necessary first step in achieving SUSTAINABLE progress in any humanitarian cause and in any fight against the world's greatest problems. If anyone reading this book has the ability to pass this book on to Jude Law, Roseanne Barr, George Clooney, Javier Bardem, Alejandro González Iñárritu, Fernando Mereilles, Shakira, Michelle Rodriguez, Matt Damon, Mos Def, Ben Affleck, Jesse Ventura, Zack de la Rocha, Brad Pitt, Ellen Degeneres, Charlize Theron, Sandra Bullock, Stephen, Damien & Ziggy Marley, Woody Harrelson, Will Smith, Queen Latifah or any other of the dozens of socially-conscious celebrities that exist all over the world, I would be honored if you would do so. I believe that celebrity participation in efforts to spread the knowledge within this book will provide much needed publicity for this very noble and necessary cause in our fight to regain our economic freedoms.

A sound monetary system rising from the ashes of this crisis will greatly enhance the possibility that the ideas contained within this book become a reality. If this book has spiked your curiosity and you wish to learn more about how a gold and silver backed system can produce economic freedom and stability, please visit our blog, the link of which you can find on our website at www.smartknowledgeu.com, visit our new sound money video channel that is coming soon on our media page on this same website, our SmartKnowledgeU YouTube video channel, where you can find a six-part video that specifically relates to the content of this book, and our Twitter and Facebook accounts.

Remember, a mere 8% of awareness about the reality of our current monetary system can provide enough momentum to forever mold the world into a much better place than it is today. In this book I have only touched upon the very tip of the iceberg regarding the immorality of the banking system. If this book has not yet convinced you of the immorality of the banking system, because my soon-to-be-released second book will explore the different facets of how our corrupt banking system actively supports criminal and immoral activities in much more depth, I am sure that my second book will do the trick. I would like to leave you with this last final nugget of food to digest. It is not enough to possess newfound knowledge, for knowledge without application is useless.

Please share this knowledge with every single person in your life. If you have young children, please share this knowledge with even young children. Our schooling system has dumbed down education to make us believe that young children are not bright enough to understand the concepts in this book but I assure you that even very young children are bright enough to understand them. If you teach your kids the concepts I discuss in this book, you will discover to your delight that children as young as 10 and 11 can fully grasp and understand the information in this book. Please refer to the videos about education in the Reference page to learn more about how the elite designed "modern" education to stifle and repress a child's intellect rather than to nurture it and you will understand that a young child is very much capable of understanding complex ideas if he or she is challenged to develop thinking skills at a young age. Share this knowledge with your friends, your neighbors, your co-workers and your colleagues. As I've stated, bankers have worked tremendously hard for the last 100 years to purge all of the knowledge in this book from our history books and from our memories. Thus, we must be willing to work just as hard today to re-introduce this knowledge into the public consciousness in order to counter the massive ongoing banker propaganda campaign today.

Furthermore, we must parlay our numbers into power. Knowledge is useless if we do not convert our knowledge into power. There is no possible way one thousand corrupt immoral bankers should be able to enslave 6.8 billion people, yet we find ourselves ensnared in this very conundrum today because too many people today know about all the information in this book but yet are unwilling to do anything about it. Millions of people that "know" still continue to support the corrupt immoral banking system by remaining worker bees that feed the immoral queen bees and they continue to live their lives with their heads down and mouths shut because of fear of the repercussions for confronting immorality.

Today, we are entrapped in a system that wrongly teaches us that conformity is good and individuality is bad. We are taught to keep our heads down instead of rising up to meet the challenges of injustices we witness. Such teachings are pure rubbish. If we spend the rest of our lives each day just trying to survive under an unjust monetary system rather than progressing every day to move closer to our glorious potential for greatness, then not only will those that dwell in poverty continue to mourn, but all 6.8 billion inhabitants of this planet will continue to mourn. In addition, we will have wasted the lives and teachings of people like Martin Luther King Jr.,

Nelson Mandela, Ghandi, and countless others that sacrificed their lives to show us that we CAN triumph over evil even when evil possesses more money and resources than us. Should we choose to cease living in fear and instead actively embrace the things that scare us in our search for justice, we will all transform into beings that will achieve greatness in our lifetime. We should no longer fear the evil lords of finance, for even if they have no conscience, our collective conscience, if utilized properly, is more than strong enough to defeat them. Live positively, live with integrity, share the truth with as many people as possible, and good things will happen. I promise you this.

If we fight the immoral bankers, destroy our current immoral banking system and free humanity by implementing a sound monetary system, I believe that such an accomplishment would usher in a new Renaissance that would surpass the old Renaissance in terms of new knowledge that would be born from this age. Today we have too many young minds that desire to work for companies like Goldman Sachs and JP Morgan that produce nothing positive for humanity and that only make money by transferring wealth from others to themselves. The wealth transfer game, however, is a destructive one for society. Implement a sound monetary system, and firms like Goldman Sachs and JP Morgan will earn minimal money every year instead of earning massive amounts of money. Insurance companies that merely transfer wealth will also no longer be able to pay exorbitant salaries. The implementation of a sound money system will drive bright young minds away from unproductive industries in finance and banking and into productive industries. Such a development will produce unprecedented advancements in science, medicine, engineering, technology, and the arts. Always

THE GOLDEN GIFT

remember if we are willing to act upon our knowledge and the truth, our strength will reach a critical mass much more quickly than anyone among us can imagine, and in the process, stop and reverse our current destructive path and usher in an age of enlightenment. Stand in solidarity with us and we will win, no matter how difficult the struggle may be.

JS KIM

CONTACTS

Webpage: http://www.smartknowledgeu.com

E-mail: soundmoney@smartknowledgeu.com

Twitter: http://www.twitter.com/smartknowledgeu

Facebook: http://www.facebook.com/smartknowledgeu

YouTube: http://www.youtube.com/smartknowledgeu

REFERENCES

Visit

http://www.smartknowledgeu/goldengiftref.php

for a complete list of links to all articles and videos mentioned in this book.

JS KIM

"In this life the righteous are few, and the courageous fewer. Seek truth and your strength and courage will multiply in such abundance as to conquer all fears of your enemies, and to instill in your enemies, great fear of you. Put the unjust on notice, for the light of justice will rout evil from the unenlightened shadows in which it perpetually dwells..."

THE GOLDEN GIFT

www.ingramcontent.com/pod-product-compliance
Lightning Source LLC
LaVergne TN
LVHW051559070426
835507LV00021B/2659